Who is this Rock?

Who is this Rock?

Hearing the Gospel in the Rocks
and Stones of Scripture

by
Garrett Soucy

WIPF & STOCK · Eugene, Oregon

WHO IS THIS ROCK?
Hearing the Gospel In the Rocks and Stones of Scripture

Wipf & Stock
An Imprint of Wipf and Stock Publishers
199 W. 8th Ave., Suite 3
Eugene, OR 97401

www.wipfandstock.com

PAPERBACK ISBN: 978-1-5326-1917-5
HARDCOVER ISBN: 978-1-4982-4533-3
EBOOK ISBN: 978-1-4982-4532-6

Manufactured in the U.S.A.

To Siiri.

You are my heart.

And to my father and mother.

Thank you for your faithfulness to God.

Contents

Chapter 1

GREGORY OF NAZIANZUS HAS famously said of the Trinity that we cannot think of the Father without thinking of the Son and the Spirit; and we cannot think of the Son without thinking of the Father and the Spirit; and we cannot think of the Spirit without thinking of the Father and the Son. An image is conjured of the Apps page on the desktop of a computer with one icon positioned in the direct center, in full color; flanked on either side, by all the other (slightly transparent) apps that one could engage. As soon as one is brought to the center, the others reorganize around it—still visible, but in the wings.

Gregory's triad is helpful on a number of Scriptural fronts, typology being one of them. When a passage on the Lord's Supper says that in partaking we "proclaim the Lord's death until He comes" (1 Cor 11:26[1]), we must not ever think of his death as something to be considered without the resurrection and the gospel being fixed in the margins. We don't only remember his death; we do, however, remember his death as a focus during the meal. And so on.

This kind of multiplicity in our thinking is important, so that one does not become one-dimensional when viewing types and allegories in the Scriptures. According to Galatians 4, Sarah and Hagar are both historical and allegorical placeholders. Similarly, there needn't be undue pressure if a passage apparently speaks to both Christ's suffering and his resurrection. The serpent in Genesis must be read both literally and allegorically. No one believes it was merely a snake.

The ability to handle any multiplicity of textual meaning, however, does not solve the problem of understanding whether or not an Old

---

1. Unless otherwise indicated, the English Standard Version is used when citing Scripture in this book.

Testament passage is positioned to be interpreted typologically. And if it is, what is the right interpretation? If Paul had not told us that Sarah was the New Covenant and Hagar was the Old Covenant, what would keep us from interpreting Hagar as the present age and Sarah as the age to come? When we try to understand a portion of text or a concept, based on its place in a larger context, we are practicing hermeneutics. Hermeneutics has long been defined as the art and science of interpretation. Here is one of the many places in which both art and science are required to cooperate, in order to more fully benefit the student.

In order to see clearly, we need to know what we are using for a lens. In order to best understand the Old Testament, we need a healthy understanding of the historical context, the intended audience, and a bit about the author. Once we have that, however, we are best fitted to feast on the passage when we don the lens of the promises being fulfilled in Christ. Without this, we will be sorting through a mess of loose ends. A helpful maxim to remember is, "we interpret the Old Testament in light of the New Testament." Old Testament typology and redemptive history both employ a Hebrew syntax. By that, I mean that they are better understood when read from right to left—Biblical understanding begins in the clear light of the New Testament, and works its light backwards. This is why the apostles' names are on the foundation stones of the heavenly city and not the patriarchs, even though the patriarchs came first (Rev 21:14).

The fact that hermeneutics is defined as a double-helix of both art and science tells us that some people will be inclined to err in the direction of the scientific. These people are often suspicious of any artistry and imagination in the work of exegesis. They avoid the works of the church fathers who tended to not be afraid of allegory and typology. In the same manner, those who err in the direction of the artistic are often guilty of eisegesis.

A good hermeneutic is like a geometrician who can acknowledge that his math, when it is true, graphs out beautifully and accurately. Again, a good hermeneutic is like a painter who can acknowledge that her painting is more beautiful when it is true. These three ancient qualities of truth, goodness, and beauty are not pitted against each other; on the contrary, they may be the closest thing we have to an abstract analogy of the Trinity.

No doubt, many will dismiss this work as having put too much weight on the artistic leg. Some will accuse it of finding Jesus under every rock in the Old Testament. To that I can only say, "Well, not *every* rock."

Mortimer Adler says that the goal of all reading is to create syntopical thinkers.[2] By this, he means that, regardless of the text one is reading at present, one is able to make connections between countless other writings—across genres, yielding manifold applications to the conversation or text in hand. In a similar sense, the goal of this book is to create syn-textual readers of the Bible. When we learn to think, within bounds, in a typological and allegorical manner, the recognition of one character, one trait, or one motif in any passage of Scripture can then stimulate cross-textual referencing and understanding. When seen as a vast network of connected meaning, our appreciation of the Bible will only grow. As our understanding expands, in light of the continuity that exists in shared imagery throughout the text, we will love the nourishment we find in this Book that will forever dwarf us.

Of course, this is not to suggest that imaginative readings, allegory, and typology should displace a grammitico-historical method of interpretation; it should accompany it. It is my desire to practice Biblical exegesis, and to serve others from streams that have refreshed me. If the art and science are clumsy dance partners, if there is a limp from favoring the artistic leg, that is my fault. My hope is that the reader will find the water to be real, and not a mirage.

2. Adler, *How to Read a Book*, 301.

Chapter 2

So early in the morning Jacob took the stone that he had put under his head and set it up for a pillar and poured oil on the top of it. He called the name of that place Bethel, but the name of the city was Luz at the first. Then Jacob made a vow, saying, "If God will be with me and will keep me in this way that I go, and will give me bread to eat and clothing to wear, so that I come again to my father's house in peace, then the Lord shall be my God, and this stone, which I have set up for a pillar, shall be God's house. And of all that you give me I will give a full tenth to you." (Gen 28:18-22)

WHEN THE BIBLICAL PATRIARCHS are spoken of, it is firstly a reference to Abraham, Isaac, Jacob, and secondly a reference to Jacob's twelve sons. These are the generations of men from whom the nation of Israel would emerge, and more importantly, from whom the Savior of the world would emerge. All of them existed before Moses, which means that they were called by God to be the media of his will, even before the Law was expressly given, a sacrificial system established, or a tabernacle ever constructed.

Jacob is the man who would wrestle with God, and would have his name changed to "Israel." The word *israel* is an enormously packed and controversial word, but many scholars agree that its meaning seems to be related to the themes of "striving with God" and "God prevailing." The whole nation is named for this man, and all that he represents—the promise of God, given to Eve, that made its way to Abraham, to Isaac, and to Jacob—the promise that God would someday prevail, using a man to undo the brokenness of the world that was brought about by sin. Israel would be the medium of the Messiah.

But this passage, in Genesis 28, takes place before Jacob ever wrestles with the angel of God. We find him having recently deceived his father, and taken his brother Esau's inheritance by trickery. After thieving the additional blessing from his dying father, Jacob takes his mother's advice and finds distant relatives with whom to form an alliance. Esau, incidentally, does the same thing. He marries into the family of his father's half-brother, Ishmael. All of this shows us the fractalizing effects of sin. The sin of one brother against another reverberates through ages of family history, and implores long-forgotten grievances to work their dark magic of division in a new generation.

On the first night of his journey, Jacob stops to rest as the sun goes down, and he uses a stone as his pillow. In his sleep, he dreams that there is a staircase pitched between heaven and Earth, and on it he sees angels ascending and descending. This staircase, or ladder as it's sometimes called, represents an intersection of the spiritual and the Earthly. The theme of correlating the vertical and the horizontal will continue to be a crucial concept throughout Scripture, but in this event, Jacob believes that he has stumbled upon a portal into the heavenly dimension, rather than that he is looking at messianic typology. He appears more superstitious than theological. Jesus would later explain that this bridge between heaven and Earth is true only of himself. Jesus is Jacob's Ladder.

> Nathanael answered him, "Rabbi, you are the Son of God! You are the King of Israel!" Jesus answered him, "Because I said to you, 'I saw you under the fig tree,' do you believe? You will see greater things than these." And he said to him, "Truly, truly, I say to you, you will see heaven opened, and the angels of God ascending and descending on the Son of Man." (John 1:49–51)

God not only gives him this vision, but he reveals himself to Jacob. He declares himself as the God of Abraham, and he links Jacob directly to Abraham as his father. Genealogies often do this when there is something about the descendent that is to be directly equated with a specific ancestor. The Bible never uses the word grandfather. Isaac, Jacob's biological father is mentioned, but Abraham is named as the progenitor. This seems to be relevant, because the nature of the call which God puts on Jacob's life is the exact same calling as that which he put upon Abraham's. It is the promise given by God to Abraham being reiterated to the next in line.

> I am the Lord, the God of Abraham your father and the God of Isaac. The land on which you lie I will give to you and to your offspring. Your offspring shall be like the dust of the earth, and you shall spread abroad to the west and to the east and to the north and to the south, and in you and your offspring shall all the families

of the earth be blessed. Behold, I am with you and will keep you wherever you go, and will bring you back to this land. For I will not leave you until I have done what I have promised you. (Gen 28:13b–15)

Jacob seems to be more taken by the event than by God. This petty thief, running from the law, speaks in such a way as to suggest that he will give this God a try; if God comes through on his end of the deal, then Jacob will give God a cut of the yields. It will take Jacob a lifetime to increasingly understand that mission to which God was calling him, and who this God was who was doing the calling.

The fact that God says he will give Jacob the land which he is on tells us one true thing about God—he is claiming that land as is his own. Now, because God promises to give life to Jacob, and generations, and territory all over, we see that God is claiming to be the owner of a lot more than just the rock which Jacob used as a pillow; however, there is a complexity to this issue of houses and lands. Jacob has run from his house—from his father's house—and hopes to make it back there someday. This is what Jacob is hoping God will procure for him in this agreement. Jacob symbolically calls the rock "Bethel," or "the house of God." It is as though he is saying, "This place is amazing. I must be in God's house. If this is really God, I'll do what he says, as long as he ends up bringing me safe and sound back to my father's house someday."

There are two hitches with this line of thinking. Even if God intended to bring Jacob back to his father's house someday (which he does in fact do, but which is incidental to the real issue), he has already established the fact that Jacob's relevant ancestor, of whom Jacob is a son, is Abraham. We could say that God *is* calling Jacob back to his father's house, indeed; but Jacob has Isaac in his mind, and God has Abraham in his. The question that must be answered, if this is the case, is "What does *Abraham* consider to be *his* house?"

> By faith Abraham obeyed when he was called to go out to a place that he was to receive as an inheritance. And he went out, not knowing where he was going. By faith he went to live in the land of promise, as in a foreign land, living in tents with Isaac and Jacob, heirs with him of the same promise. For he was looking forward to the city that has foundations, whose designer and builder is God. (Heb 11:8–10)

So, Abraham, although given a land of promise, never lives in it as though it is not his. Of course, it is his, but he does not build a permanent home. Why? There are others who have lived like this. One thinks of the the Rechabites in Jeremiah 35. Their reason for not settling down and making themselves at home was that they were obedient to the teaching of their ancestor, Jonadab. For some reason, Jonadab saw a Faustian bargain not worth making in settling down and taking pleasure in drink. It is a safe conjecture to make that his motivation may have been the same as Abraham's—because there was a greater home and a greater pleasure for which he did not want his heart to stop yearning.

We are told in the previously cited passage from Hebrews that Abraham forgoes the right to build himself a house in order that his heart might continually yearn for a place made out of rock that God himself had laid—God's house. Now we can see the full-circle irony of Jacob calling the rock upon which he slept "God's house" and imploring God to allow him to find his way to his father's house. God has already said it: "Your father is Abraham." In light of this declaration, the answer is a resounding yes, to Jacob's question of whether he will ever make it home to his father's house. The truth is, he was already there.

In literature, heroes will often strike out from home in search of some great discovery that will give both meaning and value to their existence. Often, the plot has the hero return empty-handed so that he might find his greatest treasure to be that which he had left. Only in the act of leaving it did he come to value it. This is *not* what is happening with Jacob in our passage. In this event, our hero leaves home, already eager for the return flight. God, the greater Hero, interrupts this seemingly traditional plot to teach Jacob a valuable lesson that he did not know—that there was a home for which Jacob did not yet know to yearn, a place with which Isaac's house could not compare. Thomas Wolfe famously coined the phrase, *You Can't Go Home Again*. God raises the ante by suggesting, "You have never been home."

So, Jacob wants to go home to his father someday. God calls Abraham Jacob's father. And Abraham said the only home he wanted was God's home. Jacob calls the rock on which he slept (signifying the place where heaven and Earth met) "Bethel"—God's house. God's house is symbolized by this solitary stone that Jacob anoints with oil. God's house = the anointed stone.

In keeping with the hermeneutical principle that we interpret the old in light of the new, we can see something like an ultrasound in this

Anointed Stone. It is pregnant with the stones of God's house that are yet to come, namely two: Jesus the Christ and every single individual believer. This is not only a foreshadowing of the believer functioning as the house of God, but also the believer being one living stone in that house, built upon a more important Living Stone—who is even more the House of God. God himself would build a house of living stones, and he would build it on the Rock.

This concept of God's people being represented individually by stones is again brought out in Joshua, when the Hebrew people are crossing the Jordan into the Promised Land:

> And Joshua said to them, "Pass on before the ark of the LORD your God into the midst of the Jordan, and take up each of you a stone upon his shoulder, according to the number of the tribes of the people of Israel." (Josh 4:5)

So, we see that not only does the concept of correlating the people of God to stones exist in the Old Testament, but it carries right into the New, and beyond, even into eternity. In the book of the Revelation, there is a one-to-one correlation of the people of God and stones. It is an ancient comparison. How important that we should, in light of that, understand it in its first occurrence here in Scripture.

There is something about himself that God sees as being communicable to his people in stone, at least analogously. No doubt, the surety of his salvation constantly emerges when God himself is spoken of as a Rock. The salvation of the Rock is sure, stable, and enduring. God's people are brought into this unshakable plan—the work of the Rock of Ages.

Jacob's Bethel, then, stands as a pregnant shadow of what the house of God will be in all its glory. There, in the beginning, it is one anointed stone, but throughout the progression of revelation, Bethel is seen as a wall of stones that is one thousand five hundred miles high, long, and wide. Bethel, God's house, is Abraham's house, sparse in its beginnings, but outnumbering the starry host in its crescendo. Jacob is invited to come home, just as every living stone since then has been invited home.

There is a story about Robert Frost, stopping somewhere in the rural south to watch a farmer plow a field with his horse. Frost notices the farmer dodging and circling large rocks that are flecked throughout the pasture. The work is slow and painstaking. Finally, the farmer stops and makes his way over to the fence, against which Frost is leaning. "You know," says the poet, "in New England, we pull all those rocks and line them along the edge of the field." "Yup," says the farmer. "And I just leave 'em where God flang 'em." In one way, at least, God must be more of a New Englander, because he does not leave his stones where he has flung them. He gathers them from the corners of the world, into a house of his making. This is the promise of the gospel.

Softly and Tenderly

(Will Lamartine Thompson, 1880)

O for the wonderful love he has promised,
promised for you and for me.
Though we have sinned, he has mercy and pardon,
pardon for you and for me.

Come home, come home;
you who are weary come home;
earnestly, tenderly, Jesus is calling,
calling, O sinner, come home.

Chapter 3

Then Jacob went on his journey and came to the land of the people of the east. As he looked, he saw a well in the field, and behold, three flocks of sheep lying beside it, for out of that well the flocks were watered. The stone on the well's mouth was large, and when all the flocks were gathered there, the shepherds would roll the stone from the mouth of the well and water the sheep, and put the stone back in its place over the mouth of the well. Jacob said to them, "My brothers, where do you come from?" They said, "We are from Haran." He said to them, "Do you know Laban the son of Nahor?" They said, "We know him." He said to them, "Is it well with him?" They said, "It is well; and see, Rachel his daughter is coming with the sheep!" He said, "Behold, it is still high day; it is not time for the livestock to be gathered together. Water the sheep and go, pasture them." But they said, "We cannot until all the flocks are gathered together and the stone is rolled from the mouth of the well; then we water the sheep." While he was still speaking with them, Rachel came with her father's sheep, for she was a shepherdess. Now as soon as Jacob saw Rachel the daughter of Laban his mother's brother, and the sheep of Laban his mother's brother, Jacob came near and rolled the stone from the well's mouth and watered the flock of Laban his mother's brother. Then Jacob kissed Rachel and wept aloud. And Jacob told Rachel that he was her father's kinsman, and that he was Rebekah's son, and she ran and told her father. (Gen 29:1–12)

STILL ON THE RUN, but changed by his vision at Bethel, Jacob has found his way to the home of his mother's brother, Laban. In the providence of God, as he is seeking his uncle, he comes across a group of shepherds. He hears they are from Haran, and asks if they know Laban. One of the shepherds says, "Look, there's his daughter now," and his cousin Rachel approaches.

This girl was not simply one of Laban's daughters; she was the one for whom Jacob would end up working fourteen years, in order to marry.

There is a well of water with a stone over the opening. There are three flocks of sheep set about the well. Historians have noted that, due to the precious scarcity of water, this tradition of waiting until a number of shepherds had gathered was customary.[1] Clearly, however, it was not a custom with which Jacob was familiar. But this gathering of the flocks ensured that this huge rock, which would generally require more than one man to move, didn't need to be manipulated multiple times.

One of the first things we notice is that the stone is functioning as a valve to the life-giving stream. As the rock is adjusted accordingly, the water will be accessible or not. What was the timing of this event? It was plainly positioned in relation to the gathering of all the sheep that had up until that moment been scattered. One can hear Jacob protesting the awkwardness, in his own mind, of this fullness of time.

A convergence is taking place here, unbeknownst to either Jacob or Rachel; but a thing to which we as readers are privy. How providential is the timing here. We know that we are seeing the hand of God orchestrating the intersection of Jacob and Rachel. Now, in order to comprehend some of the profundity of providence, we have to ask the questions that will develop our sense of context. In doing so, the lines will begin to gain texture.

Jacob and Rachel are both endeavoring on their own quests of sorts. Rachel is seeking someone to roll the stone away, and thereby to help her preserve her family. Jacob is seeking a family to house him, and thereby to protect him from the deathly wages of his own sin. Interestingly enough, they each find fulfillment of their quests in one another. Jacob rolls away the stone, eventually marries Rachel, and thereby blesses the house of Laban on a number of fronts. Laban houses Jacob, but even greater than that, gives him his own house by marrying his daughters to him. Of course, Jacob is given sanctuary, and his life is spared from the vengeful machinations of his brother, Esau.

The curious junction of Jacob and Rachel, in the most tactful of romantic films, would still be seen as contrived. How could two people, searching for one another, but not knowing it, stumble upon one another with such seemingly unavoidable chance? In the romantic film they would employ the intervention of kismet, the gods, serendipity, or the unavoidable

---

1. Jamieson et al., *Commentary on the Whole Bible*, 32.

magnetism that allows the heart-seeking missile of love to always find its target.

Thankfully, we are spared the violins, because the truth is that this romance itself is merely an analogy for higher love. The finest moments of *eros* are those in which *agape* is signified. The story only concerns Jacob and Rachel finding one another in a secondary way. The real story, as is always the case with the gospel, is not found in the dialogue between the two main players, but in the environmental prop that seems to have drawn them together: the stone on the well. How easy it would be to miss this. The truth is that there is a stone that mediates the access to the water, by which they will all live. It is the stone and the water that has brought the shepherds, the sheep, Rachel, and even Jacob to conference together at this place and time. There is no fate or destiny in any of it, whatsoever. It is the sovereignty of God, and it is the depth of his design into which we are inquiring.

Jacob is new to this area, and is learning the ways. We are told that he notices precisely how many flocks of sheep are gathered there, awaiting, whether the sheep know it or not, the rolling of the stone, so that they might drink, and, by drinking, live. Here is where the signification of Christ begins to emerge. Is there any reference in the New Testament to anything else likened to three flocks of sheep, waiting for the stone to be rolled away?

> When the Sabbath was past, Mary Magdalene, Mary the mother of James, and Salome bought spices, so that they might go and anoint him. And very early on the first day of the week, when the sun had risen, they went to the tomb. And they were saying to one another, "Who will roll away the stone for us from the entrance of the tomb?" (Mark 16:1–3)

Just as Jacob is surprised at the timing of the watering of the flock, when no one would expect it, so the rolling away of Jesus' stone catches the three women off guard who have come to embalm the body. Here are three lambs, knowing that the One who called himself the Living Water lay behind the rock. But they know they cannot move the stone. Nevertheless, they come to this place in order to honor the Lord, but first, they must move the stone. Why come, without the means to move the stone? It is a sign of faith, just as every migration to the watering hole was an act of faith on Rachel's behalf. What have they come to the stone to do? They must have intended to wait. Perhaps, they would implore the Lord to send someone. And, remarkably, the Lord had already sent someone.

Jacob notes that the schedule of the watering does not make sense to him, and yet the shepherds acknowledge that the timing is determined by the ingathering of the sheep. In every way, it is often said that the timing of God is a crucial part of his purpose. In Galatians 4, we read that the sending of Christ into the world was in accordance with the fullness of time, apparently being meted out by a heavenly clock.

Many people have conjectured as to the nature of why the Roman occupation of Israel may have been the perfect season of human history for the Christ to be born, but the truth is that we don't know what made the time full. In both the resurrection of the Christ, and the first meeting of Jacob and Rachel, it is appropriate to note that in accordance with God's sovereign oversight, the rock would be moved and the sheep would receive life-giving water. This is true, whether or not we can answer the question, "Why now?" The real lambs are the people who will drink of the real and living water. This is even signified in the translation of Rachel's name: "ewe." As noted, the orchestration is almost unbelievable, and yet it is absolutely believable because it is an arrangement made by the Eternal. In the New Testament, one of the most pointed explanations of God's timing is given in reference to the work of Christ and his bringing together the things of heaven and the things of Earth. This means that Christianity is not Gnosticism. It is not a spiritual reality that is no earthly good. On the contrary, it is a spiritual reality that is Earth's only hope:

> In Him we have redemption through His blood, the forgiveness of sins, according to the riches of His grace which He made to abound toward us in all wisdom and prudence, having made known to us the mystery of His will, according to His good pleasure which He purposed in Himself, that in the dispensation of the fullness of the times He might gather together in one all things in Christ, both which are in heaven and which are on earth—in Him. (Eph 1:7–10)

Not only this, but the gospel of Christ proclaims the news that he has also brought together two profoundly different people in order to make one people. The Gentiles and the Jews were like a people who were far off, and a people who were nearby. They were brought together in order to make a brand-new people:

> But now in Christ Jesus you who once were far off have been brought near by the blood of Christ. For he himself is our peace, who has made us both one and has broken down in his flesh the

dividing wall of hostility by abolishing the law of commandments expressed in ordinances, that he might create in himself one new man in place of the two, so making peace, and might reconcile us both to God in one body through the cross, thereby killing the hostility. And he came and preached peace to you who were far off and peace to those who were near. For through him we both have access in one Spirit to the Father. So then you are no longer strangers and aliens, but you are fellow citizens with the saints and members of the household of God. (Eph 2:13–19)

Perhaps we could think of Jacob and Rachel as a type of this Christ-wrought union. The first indicator that this might even be possible would be in the etymology of their names: Rachel and Jacob. Rachel, in addition to being a shepherdess, as we are told, has a name that means "ewe." Jacob, on the other hand, means something like "cheater." Imagine if the union were called out strictly by the definition of their names: "Little Lamb, you'll be paired up with the deceiver." It's counterintuitive, to say the least. And yet, this is clearly the plan of God. He would, undoubtedly, make a people for himself, from this union, and give it a new name. This is the inception of Israel which we are viewing.

One can't help but wonder if Jesus had this story of Jacob and Rachel in the back of his mind when he commissioned Peter to tend his lambs. "Look," we can imagine him saying, "The stone is rolled away and water is available, freely for all who thirst. Water Rachel's sheep. Tend my lambs."

Jacob's love for Rachel, at this point, is vicarious. He does not know Rachel personally. He is not weeping and kissing her because he has longed to be with her, or because he is smitten upon first sight. She represents the sanctuary he has sought. She represents a successful completion of the trajectory he had been sent on by his mother. He is in the fold of his family and he is safe. In a world where family meant obligation and sacrifice, he can expect not to die, but to live. We see this love played out in his desire to not only greet Rachel, but to care for the flock of sheep belonging to his kin as well.

As we shall see in the following chapter, if Paul can say about Horeb that the rock which followed the Israelites was actually, in a spiritual sense (and the fullest sense) Christ, then we should expect to see signs of him amongst his people both before and after Horeb. When Rachel and Jacob, the little lamb and the deceiver, both drink from the same well—the life-giving water which the heavy stone made available, upon being rolled away—they show us a picture of the gospel. They are two people whose names represent two very different things. They have been brought together in such a way that only God could receive praise for its having been accomplished. The stone is rolled away, and provision is made for the sheep.

The message has been the same for thousands of years. Every time we celebrate the resurrection, we are proclaiming this message that Rachel must have sung to her father, upon returning home: "The stone was rolled away, and our kinsman has done it."

As it was in the beginning, is now, and ever shall be.

Chapter 4

"Behold, I will stand before you there on the rock at Horeb, and you shall strike the rock, and water shall come out of it, and the people will drink." And Moses did so, in the sight of the elders of Israel. (Exod 17:6)

A SOLAR ECLIPSE IS an event in which the brilliance of the sun is obscured by the presence of that rock we call the moon. The difference between a solar eclipse and this event in Exodus 17 is that *this* rock in question functions as a vehicle by which God is seen, not one by which he is obfuscated.

Israel has just experienced hunger in the wilderness and subsequently been given bread from heaven. Now, they have come to Rephidim, which means "places of rest," but rest eludes them because of their thirst. Combatively, the people become obstinate and argue with Moses.

So, with petition in hand, Moses approaches God imploringly as to what he should do. God tells him to take the staff, the one with which he had struck the Nile River, and strike the rock at Horeb when God's presence rests upon the rock. There is a connection between the Nile River and this rock at Horeb, but in order to sufficiently investigate it, one should first understand a simple principle.

Speaking of the Old Testament, Augustine said, "it was then the time for concealing the grace, which had to be revealed in the New Testament by the death of Christ,—the rending, as it were, of the veil."[1] The principle is this: in the Old Testament, grace was concealed in a great way; in the New Testament, grace is revealed because Christ is revealed. We use the light of the New Testament to search for the gospel in the Old.

When a writer of the New Testament, under the inspiration of the Holy Spirit, exegetes another passage of Scripture, especially one from the

1. Augustine, *The Anti-Pelagian Writings,* 175.

Old Testament, this explanative passage of Scripture becomes foundational to our understanding of that interpreted passage. It is a simple case of the Spirit preaching his own Word. Truly, when the Bible is studied in this manner, with lines crossing from covenant to covenant, and verses stacked on top of each other, it is experienced as a pulsing and living thing. Thankfully, Paul gives us this interpretive key in relation to our passage:

> For I do not want you to be unaware, brothers, that our fathers were all under the cloud, and all passed through the sea, and all were baptized into Moses in the cloud and in the sea, and all ate the same spiritual food, and all drank the same spiritual drink. For they drank from the spiritual Rock that followed them, and the Rock was Christ. (1 Cor 10:1–4)

Back to the Nile. When Moses, seeking instruction, brings the disturbance to God, he is told that he is to take his staff with him and pass in front of the people. The people are to bear witness to the fact that God has a plan and it is being enacted. There is one qualifier which stands out. What qualifier is that? It is the specification of the staff. Moses is not allowed to bring just any staff, but it is to be the staff with which he struck the Nile River.

> And the Lord said to Moses, "Pass on before the people, taking with you some of the elders of Israel, and take in your hand the staff with which you struck the Nile, and go. (Exod 17:5)

In order to see why the qualification is given, we should inquire a bit more about the way in which the staff was used, in this Egyptian event being referenced by God. What is it that struck the Nile? Of course, the staff of Moses struck the river. But, from whence cometh the striking? It was the wrath of God. More specifically, it was the wrath of God over sin that struck the Nile. It was God's wrath over idolatry, injustice, and rebellion that caused him to strike the Nile. The staff was merely an outward sign of an inward and spiritual reality.

By telling us one of the most important facts about the Old Testament—that the Rock at Horeb was actually Christ—Paul has given us a legend by which we can navigate an understanding of the Nile/Horeb connection, and a host of other passages. The Rock from which Israel drank was Christ. Taking this into consideration, along with what he will go on to say in verse 11 of the same chapter, the basic framework needed for understanding Israel's relationship with God in the wilderness wanderings is erected. And a basic understanding of Israel's relationship with God is important, because it was written down in order to teach New Testament Christians about God.

> Now these things happened to them as an example, but they were written down for our instruction, on whom the end of the ages has come. (1 Cor 10:11)

What a strange and powerful statement. The history of Israel, and the interactions of the people of God with every circumstance that had beset them, was purposed by the Creator to be used as a physical vehicle for a spiritual understanding of life with God. As if this was not enough, the primary audience was a people who would come much further down the timeline. How humbling. Israel of old, we could see, was designed as a prototype of a newer and fuller Israel that would include people from all over the world. There is a way, Paul tells us, that the history of Israel is an instruction manual for New Covenant believers. This was not simply done by housing the law and prophets, but by physically framing with their very lives the glory of the invisible God.

With these things in mind, why does God lead Moses to this spot called Horeb? The word means *desert*. Literally, he has led Moses to the Rock in the desert. Henry Law, concerning this Rock, says, "It is a mass of mighty strength. The lashing billows lash in vain. The raging storm stirs not its fixed repose. All changing ages find it still unchanged . . . The falling sparrow and the tottering throne, the fading leaf, and the declining empire, obey a fixed resolve. His purpose cannot be moved. He is a Rock."[2]

In other words, God chose a Rock in the desert because, as Paul informed us, it is Christ. He leads them to his presence on the stone because stone shows his immutability. The presence of the Creator will dwell on one of the most lifeless forms of creation. He commands the staff to be used in violence against the stone because one cannot injure a stone; and yet, the presence of God will dwell on the Rock, and the Rock will be stricken, smitten, and afflicted. And the people will drink from the wound in his side.

> Who led you through the great and terrifying wilderness, with its fiery serpents and scorpions and thirsty ground where there was no water, who brought you water out of the flinty rock? (Deut 8:15)

---

2. Law, *The Gospel in Exodus*, 98.

This is not merely a story in which God is the Afflicted; God is the Afflictor as well. It was A. W. Tozer who once said, "We must take refuge from God in God."[3]

God hears the cries of his people and he quenches their thirst with his own blood. It is for this reason that blood and water flowed out of Christ's side together on Calvary: his work on the cross is not only efficacious for the forgiveness of sin, but he also satisfies our longing. Leonard Ravenhill used to say that this was the greatest confusion people experienced in relation to a Biblical understanding of Communion. It's not that the wine is truly blood; rather, the greater reality is that his blood is truly wine.

There is a related principle that emerges in these passages surrounding Horeb. It would be clunky and problematic to argue that there was a moment in which Christ transubstantiated into stone, despite the fact that Paul says that the Rock was Christ. The reality is that the literalness of the rock must be held in tension with an accompanying spiritual reality—no different than a snake with an unmentioned spiritual entity accompanying it or bread and wine in remembrance of Christ. The literal vehicle is real. The accompanying presence is real. The spiritual slaking is as real as the literal. A person may come to God, not only for forgiveness, but satiation. When Jesus announces this on the last day of the feast, there must be no doubt that he is the Rock of God, inviting the thirsty to drink, as he did in the desert. Horeb must be in his mind:

> On the last day of the feast, the great day, Jesus stood up and cried out, "If anyone thirsts, let him come to me and drink. (John 7:37)

Finally, there is one more note that needs examination. When the line finally dies down and everyone has had a chance to drink their fill, Moses names the place. Rephidim and Horeb are names that already existed; but the naming that Moses does has to do with the events that presently had unfolded in that place. He does not name it once, but twice. There are two great moments of consequence that occur: a quarreling on Israel's part amongst themselves, and a testing of the Lord.

Quarreling children of God and a testing of the Lord often go hand in hand. One can imagine that if some group of professing believers have given themselves over to infighting, it would be quite natural for them to have also given themselves over to doubting the sovereignty of God. At the core of all murmuring is unbelief. We complain because we assume

---

3. Tozer, *The Knowledge of the Holy*, 107.

there must have been a mistake. We argue because we assume we've been wronged. We keep murmuring and arguing because we assume God must not have heard us. The only other option in the rebellious and unbelieving mind is that he has heard us and does not care. And this is where we find the people of Israel. Thousands of years later, we will find them there again:

> On that day, when evening had come, he said to them, "Let us go across to the other side." And leaving the crowd, they took him with them in the boat, just as he was. And other boats were with him. And a great windstorm arose, and the waves were breaking into the boat, so that the boat was already filling. But he was in the stern, asleep on the cushion. And they woke him and said to him, "Teacher, do you not care that we are perishing?" And he awoke and rebuked the wind and said to the sea, "Peace! Be still!" And the wind ceased, and there was a great calm. He said to them, "Why are you so afraid? Have you still no faith?" And they were filled with great fear and said to one another, "Who then is this, that even the wind and the sea obey him?" (Mark 4:35–41)

Imagine for a moment that we are watching a film of these two events on a split screen. On one side are the thirsty Israelites complaining to Moses that he could care less that they are dying. On the other side are the Israelites complaining to Jesus that he could care less that they are dying. In both instances, the word of God had been issued, that he would take them to the place to which they were journeying:

> Go and gather the elders of Israel together and say to them, "The Lord, the God of your fathers, the God of Abraham, of Isaac, and of Jacob, has appeared to me, saying, 'I have observed you and what has been done to you in Egypt, and I promise that I will bring you up out of the affliction of Egypt to the land of the Canaanites, the Hittites, the Amorites, the Perizzites, the Hivites, and the Jebusites, a land flowing with milk and honey.'" (Exod 3:16–17)

> On that day, when evening had come, he said to them, "Let us go across to the other side." (Mark 4:35)

Both sets of accusations against God rest entirely on one or both of the two options: God is not there, or God does not care. The reality, of course, is that murmuring is unbelief. The word of God is sure, and in both cases the word of God had been delivered. The illusion that God was asleep, or aloof, or sinister is just that—an illusion. Jesus is not sleeping because he couldn't care less, but because he is convinced that God cares intimately; therefore he can sleep. The disciples wanted the peace of Rome, not the peace of Christ. They wanted escape from the storm, not perseverance through it. They wanted the fragile vessel kept out of harm's way, which is to say that they did not want God to receive glory for doing what would otherwise be impossible. Murmuring is unbelief. Christ was asleep because he knew God cared, and that God was sovereign. When Israel thirsted, Christ had not withheld water from them because he is a scoundrel; rather, he withheld water to teach them to trust him. The suffering was for the perfecting of faith, but they would have none of it.

Look. We are told that the Rock is Christ. God is before his people. He is struck per his own ordination, and the people of God drink freely from his riven side. And all this in response, not to their worship of him, but their quarreling and rebellion. There is no charge that can be brought against God, other than that of him being merciful and gracious.

Glorious things of Thee are Spoken

(John Newton, 1779)

Glorious things of thee are spoken,
Zion, city of our God.
God, whose word cannot be broken,
formed thee for his own abode.
On the Rock of Ages founded,
what can shake thy sure repose?
With salvation's walls surrounded,
thou may'st smile at all thy foes.

See, the streams of living waters,
springing from eternal love,
well supply thy sons and daughters
and all fear of want remove.
Who can faint while such a river
ever flows their thirst to assuage?
Grace, which like the Lord, the giver,
never fails from age to age.

Chapter 5

But Moses' hands grew weary, so they took a stone and put it under him, and he sat on it, while Aaron and Hur held up his hands, one on one side, and the other on the other side. So his hands were steady until the going down of the sun. And Joshua overwhelmed Amalek and his people with the sword. (Exod 17:12–13)

THERE IS SOMETHING ADDICTIVE about the work of ancestry recovery. Rarely is the myriad of narratives that was woven together to make us who we are talked about in detail. One are two generations back is often the limit of our capacity to name our ancestors. Imagine if it you were to find out that a notable person had been discovered in your ancestry. Imagine if it were someone you'd never heard of, but someone with a story that others have remembered. It is the most natural thing in the world to begin to read about this person, even to hunt down photographs and crane one's neck at different angles in front of the mirror to see if we can find the resemblance.

Moses is an ancestor of all true believers. God used him to preach about himself to those who are able to hear the sermon. In this Exodus passage, Moses is positioned by God into a crucible of sorts. It is in this strange posture that God will proclaim down the corridor of time the message that, in order to experience the victory of God, we must live in dependency on God.

Immediately after the event at the Rock of Horeb, the Scriptures take us to a battle between the Amalekites and the Israelites. The battle takes place in Rephidim, the region in which Israel was already camped, where God brought water from the rock.

Remembering how God had used his staff to repeatedly broker great outcomes, Moses tells Joshua to choose some men to go into the valley and engage Amalek, while he will place himself on the hill, overlooking the valley, staff in hand.

The Amalekites were relatives of the Israelites. This makes the attack so much more than an ambush from local infidels. We are told in Genesis 36 that Amalek is a grandson of Esau. These descendants of Esau travel out of Canaan and attack Israel without provocation. Many assume that the idea behind their offensive would be to try to gain the upper hand on this legendary people by attacking Israel before they make their way to Canaan and displace them. God will not forget this attack, as is clear in the closing verses of Exodus 17, but also in the remembrance of it in Deuteronomy. The attack, according to God, was a direct assault against the Creator. They didn't fear God, we are told. Family traditions die hard. For this reason, Israel was being prepared to move into the land and destroy the remnant of this and other wicked people groups.

When Moses begins to grow weary, the two men who are with him, Aaron and Hur, place a rock under their leader so that he can perch himself atop it, while the men each position themselves on either side of the old man, in order to hold up his arms; for when his arms were in the air, Israel prevailed in battle, and when his arms would drop, Amalek would prevail.

No doubt, there are times when people might be tempted to think of events like this as dubious accountings. This is not the case. Why might someone think of this scene as being riddled with superstition? Because the reader is supposed to believe that when an old man held a magic stick in the air, one army would prevail over another. It can sound childish and uncivilized. The truth is that we are not dealing with magic. We are dealing with a God whose actions are not only powerful but didactic. He is not simply proving himself, but he is teaching all generations about himself.

What is the teaching in this battle? What is the promise we conflate with the power? Can it be that the gospel is being preached to believers, generations after this event, in the details of the account?

Firstly, we would be amiss to not recognize that this is the second time in this chapter that someone has perched themselves atop a rock. Only a few verses prior, as we saw in the last chapter, God told Moses that he would place himself atop the Rock just prior to Moses' striking it. This was done so that the message being proclaimed down the hall of time would reverberate loud and clear. Paul tells us that the message was that Jesus was the Rock. For those who believe that the Son is co-eternal with the Father, this not only makes perfect sense, but it helps us to see the gospel cohesion in all of Scripture.

Now, just six short verses later, Moses is placed atop a rock. To have been given such gospel insight into the similar event at Horeb by Paul, and to then miss the gospel symbolism taking place in this battle with Amalek, would be tragic.

Is there a consistent Biblical description of how God uses the concept of the rock, and if it were to be applied in this passage, would the motif retain consistency? Clearly, the intent of this book is to show that this is the case, but, to begin with, see what David says, per the inspiration of the Holy Spirit:

> The LORD is my rock and my fortress and my deliverer, my God,
> my rock, in whom I take refuge, my shield, and the horn of my
> salvation, my stronghold. (Ps 18:2)

This is a warrior, speaking of God as a rock, and by that he means success in battle. Incontrovertibly, David's warrior terminology extends far beyond literal war, even in his own day, although it does include literal war; however, in the New Covenant, the warrior analogies are applied literally to the truer and only still-standing enemies: spiritual strongholds. New Covenant believers can sing the imprecatory Psalms, but they must sing them against lust and greed . . . not Assyrians nor Persians. David, being a true believer in the Old Covenant, employs a mix of the literal and the spiritual.

The epitome of a successful battle would not only be the efficient conquering of one's enemies, but also the successful protection of one's own peoples. The latter is being sung about in the above-cited Psalm. On all sides, David says that God has been a Fortress, a Deliverer, a Refuge, a Shield, a Savior, and a Stronghold. He references God as being all these things in one word which he repeats: Rock.

Now, we see Moses, the leader of the people of God, stationed upon the rock, and a direct relationship emerging between this and the victory over their enemies. But this is not the only thing taking place. They are not only being kept safe and delivered from their own deaths, but they are winning the battle as well:

> For who is God, but the Lord? And who is a rock, except our
> God?—the God who equipped me with strength and made my
> way blameless. He made my feet like the feet of a deer and set me
> secure on the heights. He trains my hands for war, so that my arms
> can bend a bow of bronze. You have given me the shield of your
> salvation, and your right hand supported me, and your gentleness
> made me great. You gave a wide place for my steps under me, and

my feet did not slip. I pursued my enemies and overtook them,
and did not turn back till they were consumed. (Ps 18:31–37)

The only Rock that exists, is God, says David. He then goes on to describe, in the very same chapter, how God is not only a Rock who saves his people from their enemies, but he is a Rock who crushes the enemies of his people. Those who love to sneak and set traps, David says further on in Solomonic fashion, will be devoured by them. Such is the case with Amalek. Moses is seated on the Rock, and the battle is being won for the people of God. Moses is stayed on the Rock, and the Rock is undoubtedly the Rock of Salvation.

But the Rock upon which Moses sits is only part of the gospel message. There are other pieces built into it. Moses is seated on the Rock, but his arms are held up by other men from the camp. His arms are held up; his staff is in his hand; and Moses is growing weary.

The man of God, in this Exodus passage, is a mighty leader. He is a Bible hero unparalleled. But what is the message in this passage? The victory is not only related to the man of God being established on the Rock, but it is required of him that he remain in a posture of surrender and dependency. To fail to do so is to lose the battle. Aaron and Hur are not commissioned to cheer him on. They are commissioned to hold his arms up. What curious irony. The leader of the people exists in a perpetual state of surrender, that by doing so they might be victorious in battle. The only way this makes sense is to place it all under the rubric of gospel logic. Every person who surrenders to Christ is truly victorious:

Truly, I say to you, unless you turn and become like children, you
will never enter the kingdom of heaven. (Matt 18:3b)

After the event at Horeb, Moses renamed the place, and he gave it two names. One name meant *quarreling* and one name meant *testing*. The quarreling commemoration was made because the people fought with one another and with Moses. Even down to this day, it is remembered of them that they complained and argued. The other name was given because the people tested God. Moses even says in what manner they did such a thing:

And he called the name of the place Massah and Meribah, because
of the quarreling of the people of Israel, and because they tested
the Lord by saying, "Is the Lord among us or not?" (Exod 17:7)

What they had done to test the Lord was to question whether or not he was still among them. And so, Moses stands with his hands raised in surrender to the Lord, and Israel wins. Imagine the shock and fear that must have raced through him when he made the connection between their success of the troops and the position of his hands. Moses is showing us what it looks like not only to be a godly leader, but to be a godly believer. It is to live in dependency on the Rock, both beneath us and above us.

It would have been the simplest thing in the world to deny that it is possible that his own arms being raised was the key to the success against Amalek. The simplest thing would be to confess a wave of self-centeredness and a brief encounter with the world of Messiah complexes. Moses could have slapped himself in the face a few times and asked Aaron to pinch him. What was he thinking? There is no way that a guy raising his arms in the air—or not—could determine the outcome of war. But it was not about a man raising his arms in the air or not. It was always about whether or not God was preaching the gospel through Israel for the rest of human history after him to receive. To put his arms down would have been to surrender to the unbelieving error that God must not actually be among them.

I remember a time when a woman who was not very old came down with a sudden sickness and was immediately on the brink of death. It was quite sudden and certainly a shock to the congregation. Everyone was praying for healing, despite the fact that hospice had been called in and the family had gathered to say their farewells. Remarkably, and in an unforeseen manner, this woman began to come out of the sickness and nearly as rapidly returned to a healthy form of functioning.

A friend was leading the call to worship the Sunday after this woman's recovery and she chastised the congregation. "How dare we?" she said. "How dare any of us suggest that this woman's tenacity is the cause for her recovery. How dare we use quippy sayings about us knowing *she had it in her*. We have prayed to God as our only hope, as the One who holds the power of life and death in his hands. If this woman has recovered, God alone should get the glory."

It was a prophetic rebuke. How easy it is for us to be unbelieving in reference to God's sovereignty over and involvement in the world. One could enter any number of jokes here about praying petitioners saying, "Forget it God, a helicopter is here now."

This concept of believers being people who live in dependency on God weaves through the entire Bible. We find it in the letter that Paul wrote to the church in Galatia. The primary issue with these folks is that they had started flirting with a return to the customs and traditions of Judaism. That, on its own, isn't the worst thing about their condition. The recovery of things like circumcision and food laws was most problematic because they stripped Christ from his rightful position as the fulfillment of these things, and they were rejecting the sufficiency of Christ in relation to both justification and sanctification. This Galatian error is best summed up in the following manner:

> Are you so foolish? Having begun by the Spirit, are you now being perfected by the flesh? (Gal 3:3)

The fact that Paul has to address the error in how these folks lived—after being justified—shows that the poison of a works-based righteousness has crept beyond the borders of justification and has made its way into the fabric of sanctification as well. They had forgotten the simple truth that a mature Christian was not someone who could spar with theologians in the original languages. Not at all. A mature Christian is someone who has walked with the Lord for a long time and never put their arms down. To suggest that a continuance in the faith looks different than dependency on the Spirit is foolishness, according the Spirit of God:

> By faith Moses, when he was grown up, refused to be called the son of Pharaoh's daughter, choosing rather to be mistreated with the people of God than to enjoy the fleeting pleasures of sin. He considered the reproach of Christ greater wealth than the treasures of Egypt, for he was looking to the reward. (Heb 11:24–26)

Moses is preaching a sermon to all the believers that would come after him. He is showing the church, more than anyone else, what godly leadership looks like. Firstly, it is dependent on membership in the body. Aaron was Moses' brother. Josephus, the Jewish historian, informs us that Hur was Miriam's husband, making him Moses' brother-in-law.[1] He is Caleb's son, making the kinds of lineages represented in this battle strongly contrasted. We hear about Hur a couple of times. We hear about Aaron more so. They were both men that God had given Moses to help him in leading the people of God.

Moses began to grow weary, and Aaron and Hur were the ones to place him on the rock, and to hold up his arms. They helped him show the people of God what dependency on God looked like. They came alongside

---

1. Josephus, *Antiquities Book III*, 69.

him, literally, and helped him to do his job. This is kingdom leadership. It is leadership that cannot be accomplished without help. Kingdom leadership is encompassed on all sides by dependency: Moses is seated on the Rock, hands raised to heaven, arms held up by his friends. Now we begin to see what makes Moses such a great believer, his posture is that of a child.

Here is the lesson of perseverance as well. Moses did not persevere. He was persevered. All endurance requires an external perseverant. For the believer, this is ultimately promised to be God himself.

> Being strengthened with all power, according to his glorious might, for all endurance and patience with joy; giving thanks to the Father, who has qualified you to share in the inheritance of the saints in light. (Col 1:11–12)

These hands that are being held in the air are the very hands that held the tablets of the Law. They are the hands that carried the Word of God to the people of God, and now God is fashioning them to show the people of God how to abide in him. Just as Jesus declared that the Word of God was a thing never to pass away, so the Rock stands as this fixed marker, unwavered by the years and the calamities. Should this all go on for millions of years from now, there will be men and women of God whom he raises up, who place themselves on the very same Word and will not be shaken. They will stand in the line of Moses, whom God established as an example for New Covenant believers throughout the world, of what it looks like to be shipwrecked upon the shores of the living God.

I Need Thee, Every Hour

(Annie S. Hawks, 1872)

I need thee every hour,
in joy or pain;
come quickly and abide,
or life is vain.

I need thee, O I need thee,
every hour I need thee.
O bless me now, my Savior;
I come to thee.

Chapter 6

If you make me an altar of stone, you shall not build it of hewn stones, for if you wield your tool on it you profane it. (Exod 20:25)

THERE IS A STORY that Melody Green tells in her book, *No Compromise*, about her late husband, Keith Green. They were passing a field one day and Keith made mention of how it was such a beautiful spot. Melody held her breath and waited for what would come next. Historically, he would remark that a field like that should be used to build a Bible college, or an orphanage, but this one time he made no follow-up comment. She says in the book that it was such a profound event, and one that showed that a true maturity was taking place. Keith was able to give credit to God's creativity and goodness, without needing to perfect it with his own finishing touches.[1] Beauty is sufficient in itself without a necessary utilitarian application other than pleasure. We approach something akin to this when we look at this passage in Exodus concerning the earthen altar.

An altar was a place whereupon God was worshiped. In the Old Covenant, the act of giving the best part of one's wealth, which was outwardly signified more in one's agricultural assets than anything else, was one of the primary ways in which God was worshiped. The concept that God has required that he be worshiped in certain ways, and not in others, is an intertestamental concept. There are a number of ways in which God frames prerequisites for proper worship, such as the passage in question. It is safe to say that, in the New Covenant, this regulative principle is reduced to one sharp inward requirement: worship must be done in spirit and in truth.

God is spirit, and those who worship him must worship in spirit and truth. (John 4:24)

---

1. Green, *No Compromise*, chapter 17.

There are other passages that can make sense of this, in an applicatory manner, but the primary principle is that simple maxim of Christ's. Jesus is speaking to the woman at the well. She has used the issue of the regulative principle as a divergent, in order to avoid having a conversation about her own sin. She is a great legalist in this sense. The fact remains that, in the Old Covenant, some aspects of the law carried the prophetic weight of symbolism. It's not that God actually hates blended fabrics. He hates the tepid abdication of a person whose heart serves two masters. Blended wine and blended fabric were external props by which he could teach that lesson. It is why, when the New Covenant is issued, these external props begin to lose their efficacy—because the Holy Spirit was given, and the Instructor would reign in the heart. The lesson of being single-minded would leave the skin and enter the innermost regions. We are in similar territory in our passage about the unhewn altar. Here is the Exodus line of Scripture within the context of the verses around it:

> And the Lord said to Moses, "Thus you shall say to the people of Israel: 'You have seen for yourselves that I have talked with you from heaven. You shall not make gods of silver to be with me, nor shall you make for yourselves gods of gold. An altar of earth you shall make for me and sacrifice on it your burnt offerings and your peace offerings, your sheep and your oxen. In every place where I cause my name to be remembered I will come to you and bless you. If you make me an altar of stone, you shall not build it of hewn stones, for if you wield your tool on it you profane it. And you shall not go up by steps to my altar, that your nakedness be not exposed on it.'" (Exod 20:22–26)

In this passage, the symbolism emerges as crucial, while at the same time, the literalism becomes clunky. That should be remembered. Why interject this caveat about not going up steps to the altar, in case someone isn't wearing underwear? A mocker would read this passage and, well, mock. The truth is that, if someone does not take great care in recognizing Whom it is they approach, with the purpose of giving worth that is due, then they have not understood the act of worship. There are people that will get dressed for a job interview at a fast food restaurant. Why? Because they need a job and they want to give the impression that the entire thing matters. Worship is ascribing worth to the God Whom we believe deserves being praised. For a child to chomp their gum while an adult is talking to them, or to not look the adult in the eye, is disrespectful. To not bother taking into account the symbolism of exposing my nakedness to the symbol of the God of Israel, while I offer him worship, is to disregard the symbolic nature of my duplicity. I profane the very God I claim to worship. It is far from being humorous. It's far from being pedantic. This is all about meaning. God is teaching his people to think simultaneously in multiple genres. He is teaching us to navigate the tightrope of the literal and the symbolic.

In every generation, there exists some avant-garde artist who prides himself or herself on their daring venture of blasphemy. Whether it is Jean Fouquet, Andres Serrano, or Miriam Abramovich, the only reason that Christians are offended and shocked when vile things are done to sacred symbols is, not because our God has been injured, but because a symbol that represents our God has been used to show the bent of a rebellious pagan heart—and, most importantly, this was done in opposition to the truth that our God deserves worship. Blasphemy says, "death to God." The pagan has made a statement about our God, via symbolism. God has more of a right than any artist to demand symbolic integrity. Obviously, Christians do not believe that divine things should be handled in a haphazard manner. That is precisely what the Exodus passage is teaching. We are to worship God as he is and not fashion him according to our inclinations.

The God of Israel chose to identify himself, and have his people signify him, with rock. There is no shortage of examples proving this. When God distinguishes himself from the false gods of Israel's neighbors, he points out that he will not let them fashion a gold or silver statue of any god, let alone himself. In fact, the very altar upon which they will sacrifice to God must be made of earth and unhewn stones. This is a blatant contrast to the polished precious metal that has been shaped by a fallen imagination.

> You shall not make gods of silver to be with me, nor shall you make for yourselves gods of gold. An altar of earth you shall make for me and sacrifice on it your burnt offerings and your peace offerings, your sheep and your oxen. (Exod 20:23)

Consistently, God identifies himself with rock, and contrasts it with other elemental vehicles. In Exodus 20, it is in direct contrast with the role of man as maker. If God the Father were to allow an image made of him, even a beautiful one, he would be abdicating the role of God to the artist, and assuming the role of the created or made one. A rock, as one finds it, is such a counter-intuitive prop when one is dealing with God. If the Creator of the universe is to eat dinner at your house, you wouldn't serve the meal on paper plates. When David realizes that he has built himself a mansion, and the presence of God is being stored in the garage, he impulsively and understandably decides to build God a better mansion than his. When we read God's response, however, it's as if God says, "Eh. I'd rather sleep outside." God requires the altar of unhewn stone, an altar of earth, to remind us that He's not like us. All of these paleo-aesthetics train the worshiper of the One True God to come to him in reliance on hearing and not on sight. This is a gift from the God who cannot be seen, and whose Son is called The Word.

The French thinker Jacques Ellul says that images belong to an entirely different family than words. When we say that a picture is worth a thousand words, notice that no one ever qualifies what kind of words. By their very nature, words limit what kind of pictures may be conjured.

> I repeat, that of course not all images are idolatrous and demonic. But they are in effect opposed to the word, belong to another order, and are intrinsically contradictory and not complementary to the word.[2]

Because God identifies with rock, there is a "nothing to see here" anticlimax that will be experienced if someone has come to this God in order to see something comparable to what idols are ever so willing to show. As Ellul says, by so doing, God postures his worshipers in such a manner that they come to the Rock eager to hear. And this is an appropriate approach, because, while this God has not shown us his face, he most certainly has spoken. To come to the Rock in a desirous way is to crane our necks toward his word. We are to approach with our ears open, not our eyes:

> To you, O LORD, I call; my rock, be not deaf to me, lest, if you be silent to me, I become like those who go down to the pit. (Ps 28:1)

David knows God to be a God of the word. Of course God sees us as well. He sees all things. His vision is perfect. The reason for David's pleading with God to hear him is because he is referring to him as the Rock. He is acknowledging that God's is the central and primary perspective that matters. Approaching the invisible God via sight is to say that we are the fixed point, viewing God from the position of the interpreter. We may not mean to do this, but it is unavoidable if we are not approaching God through his Word. Such a person says, "This is how I see God." They do not say, "This is

---

2. Ellul, *The Humiliation of the Word*, 91.

how God has declared himself." It is for this reason, God elicits the warning about taking any tool to the altar:

> If you make me an altar of stone, you shall not build it of hewn stones, for if you wield your tool on it you profane it. (Exod 20:25)

There is no greater offense to the will of man than the living God. We find God like an unhewn stone. We are confident that he will become invaluable to us, somehow. But, as we attempt to utilize him, we find that his shape will not conform to any of our categories. He is obtuse. He is abrasive. He is unwilling to bend. And so, many do what seems to be right in their own eyes: they take out a chisel and hammer, and they salvage what they can of this Ancient Anachronism, so that a generation might not assign him part and parcel to the trash heap. In their minds, they rescue God. They have made him straighter and more even keeled. But in doing so, they have remade him. He is now fit for mass production.

When the Scripture says that to take a chisel to the altar stone is to profane it, the idea is to render it unfit for sacred use. Some translations say that it is thusly polluted. But, according to Brown, Driver, and Briggs, profane is actually the third definition of the word חלל.[3] The first definition means to bore a hole into, or to pierce. The idea is that to take a chisel to the stone is to have wrecked it. How did they profane God? They pierced the Rock of God.

The truth is that if we had the chance to fashion God, we would not stop at trimming his nails. We would not stop chipping away until we saw our own face in the rock. Part of this is due to how the Fall has mutilated the *Imago Dei*; part of it is the sinful desire we inherited from Adam to usurp God. It is as Voltaire has said, "If God has made us in his image, we have returned him the favor."[4]

We need look no further than the parables of Jesus to realize that good things can become sin to those whose hearts reject the gospel. In the parable of the prodigal son, the older brother is the only one who won't partake in the feast at the end of the parable. The reason he refuses to partake is because sinners are at the table, and he's been too good to ruin his reputation now by getting grace all over it. Tim Keller says it this way:

> The elder brother is not losing the father's love in spite of his goodness, but because of it. It is not his sins that create the barrier

3. Brown, *The Brown-Driver-Briggs Hebrew and English Lexicon*.
4. Voltaire, *Notebooks*.

between him and his father, it's the pride he has in his moral record; it's not his wrongdoing but his righteousness that is keeping
him from sharing in the feast of the father.[5]

All this is to say that, of course, there is a way to do the correct thing
sinfully. When God, during Isaiah's day, explains the reasons for the coming judgment, he calls to the stand the fact that they are doing things the
correct way, but their heart is not in it. They approached him "correctly" in
an outward fashion, but the twisted nature of the inward reality disqualified
them from being true worshipers of God:

> And the Lord said: "Because this people draw near with their
> mouth and honor me with their lips, while their hearts are far
> from me, and their fear of me is a commandment taught by men,
> therefore, behold, I will again do wonderful things with this peo-
> ple, with wonder upon wonder; and the wisdom of their wise men
> shall perish and the discernment of their discerning men shall be
> hidden." (Isa 29:13–14)

This is the beauty of the transition that has taken place in the advent of
the New Covenant: true worship may outwardly look different. If one were
to watch a group of Christians worshiping God on a hot summer night,
crammed into a barn in rural Vietnam, it would look very different from
the scene taking place on a Sunday morning, in a little white church in
Liberty, Maine. In either location, any disqualification that is made is issued
over the condition of the heart. The principle still exists: God has no need
of interpreters, let alone redactors. Isaiah's Israel, by worshiping incorrectly,
was guilty of usurping God. They believed themselves to be sufficient to
stand at the altar of God and say, "This rock is not very even. I can fix that."

> You turn things upside down! Shall the potter be regarded as the
> clay, that the thing made should say of its maker, "He did not make
> me"; or the thing formed say of him who formed it, "He has no
> understanding"? (Isa 29:16)

God's requirement for worship is a truthful and spiritual heart. To approach him on any other terms is to defy his authority. We profane him
when we approach him flippantly. We pierce him with our irreverence. God
has said how we are to approach him. We must hear him and obey. We must
begin with the utterance, "Hallowed be Thy Name."

---

5. Keller, *The Prodigal God*, 34.

CHAPTER 6

God Moves in a Mysterious Way

(William Cowper, 1774)

God moves in a mysterious way
His wonders to perform;
He plants His footsteps in the sea
And rides upon the storm.
Deep in unfathomable mines
Of never failing skill
He treasures up His bright designs
And works His sov'reign will.
Ye fearful saints, fresh courage take;
The clouds ye so much dread
Are big with mercy and shall break
In blessings on your head.
Judge not the Lord by feeble sense,
But trust Him for His grace;
Behind a frowning providence
He hides a smiling face.
His purposes will ripen fast,
Unfolding every hour;
The bud may have a bitter taste,
But sweet will be the flow'r.
Blind unbelief is sure to err
And scan His work in vain;
God is His own interpreter,
And He will make it plain.

Chapter 7

And he gave to Moses, when he had finished speaking with him on Mount Sinai, the two tablets of the testimony, tablets of stone, written with the finger of God. (Exod 31:18)

THE GIVING OF THE Law could be seen as a very cold and calculated transaction. The reputation of the Law is rightly one of precision and an unforgiving exactitude. How is it that Old Testament believers, like David, could say that they loved the Law, when it's job was to condemn and kill? It is possible that there is something in the Law that prophecies grace. There is something in the Law that declares the character of a God that would himself pay for the guilt of his people.

In this chapter of Exodus, God has already spoken the Law to Moses; but, before Moses returns to the people, the Lord informs him about having called Bezalel and Oholiab to be artists in his service. These two men are the first people mentioned in Scripture as being "filled with the Spirit of God." Their story is perhaps the greatest endorsement of God issuing a call for people to work normal jobs as worship to the Lord. God himself filled these men with the Holy Spirit so that they could be artists, carpenters, and stonecutters to his glory. They were not sons of Aaron. They would not be ministers in the Tabernacle; but they would help build the Tabernacle and all the things in it. They were not described as men who were chosen on the basis of their strengths. They were men that God specifically gifted to do this work. In a world where so many people are clocking into jobs, but wish they could be serving the Lord in a ministerial fashion, Bezalel and Oholiab's calling shows us that what is often needed is not a change of profession, but a change of perspective. No doubt, God may have gifted these men from birth. They may have been at the top of their class. These things do not negate the sovereign hand of God in having chosen them for this service, and having gifted them beforehand. Their spiritual gifting was to do normal work well.

In addition, their enlistment functions as a safeguard, to keep people from running further than is appropriate on the trajectory of the word superseding the image. With God, the word, most assuredly, always takes primacy over the image; however, a hyperextension of this thought would be to suggest that God rejects all images. God has chosen unhewn rock, thus far, with which to identify himself. But, as the writer of Hebrews explains, the crafted furniture within the tabernacle, and even the engineered tabernacle itself, preaches Christ and his gospel. They are not discarded, because they have been melted, shaped, and hewn. But it is rock and stone that he consistently employs in a self-referential manner.

> Thus it was necessary for the copies of the heavenly things to be purified with these rites, but the heavenly things themselves with better sacrifices than these. For Christ has entered, not into holy places made with hands, which are copies of the true things, but into heaven itself, now to appear in the presence of God on our behalf. (Heb 9:23–24)

In Exodus 31, Moses has already been given the Law, but he is still on the mountain. He is informed about Bezalel and Oholiab, and then God turns his attention to the concept of Sabbath. Almost as a reminder, he says that Sabbath-keeping should be the one thing the Jewish people are marked by, more than anything else.

God himself hews the stone tablets and writes the commandments on them. Later, after Moses' anger causes him to break both tablets of the Law, God requires Moses to hew new tablets, but the Lord inscribes the commandments again.

"And He gave to Moses," the verse says. God gives his own Law to Moses, that Moses might give it to the people on God's behalf. He is the visible mediator for the Invisible God. This bequeathing of authority will be a point of respect in the hearts of believing Israel, and a bullseye on Moses' back in the eyes of the rebels. Those who recognize God as the giver of the authority will honor Moses as the mediator of the covenant. Those who don't will see Moses as a megalomaniac. Even before the giving of the Law, God had called Moses into his mediatorial role, when he called him out of Egypt.

During the battle with Amalek, as well, God positions Moses in such a way that he is forced to copy the posture of God. At Horeb, God told

Moses that he would place himself upon the Rock and then Moses was to strike it. In the battle with Amalek, just after the incident with the Rock at Horeb, Moses is raising his arms and is forced to sit atop a rock. This was the position of God just prior to the battle with the Amalekites in the very same chapter. Moses is given the role of being a diplomat for God.

> And the LORD said to Moses, "See, I have made you like God to Pharaoh, and your brother Aaron shall be your prophet. (Exod 7:1)

To represent God to the world makes his leaving the palatial halls of Egypt not seem so costly; though it was a role that would, in fact, cost him dearly. He was the mediator between God and man.

> He shall speak for you to the people, and he shall be your mouth, and you shall be as God to him. (Exod 4:16)

No wonder the prophecies of Moses, concerning the Christ, tell the people to look for someone who was like him. Moses, on so many fronts, was a type of Christ. There can, however, be no doubt that Christ was the One greater than Moses.

> The Lord your God will raise up for you a prophet like me from among you, from your brothers—it is to him you shall listen—just as you desired of the Lord your God at Horeb on the day of the assembly, when you said, "Let me not hear again the voice of the Lord my God or see this great fire any more, lest I die." And the Lord said to me, "They are right in what they have spoken. I will raise up for them a prophet like you from among their brothers. And I will put my words in his mouth, and he shall speak to them all that I command him. And whoever will not listen to my words that he shall speak in my name, I myself will require it of him." (Deut 18:15–19)

This authority that was given by God to Moses will be regularly tested. He is about to issue the Law. Imagine any given person in a far less serious role, nevertheless, having to be the one to insist on protocol. That person is despised. The resident assistant in a college dorm, the parking enforcement officer, the movie theater usher, the preacher, and the customer service operator: rebels of every age have postured themselves against anyone representing authority. How much more so was this the case with Moses, who was chosen to deliver what Paul would later call "a law of sin and death" (Rom 8)? Yet, deliver it he must.

The church has recognized for a very long time that the Law was derived directly from the person of God, and does not exist as something outside of him. The Law was not some ancient rule that binds even the Creator. It is best to understand the Law as a signifying derivative of God's character. This is seen most plainly in the manner in which God issues the Law. It is on tablets of stone. As has been said, God has chosen, quite consistently, to employ rock and stone in a self-referential manner. If the Law is derived from the character of God, then it makes perfect sense the the tablets would be hewn from stone.

God's timing, in this regard, is rooted in his omniscience. By the time he sends Moses down the mountain, with the Law, the people have commissioned Aaron into melting down their earrings and crafting the golden calf. The stone tablets stand in opposition to the golden calf on a number of fronts. For one, the tablets are stone which has been hewn by God. In keeping with our analysis, this would mean that God is giving the Law from himself. The golden calf, on the other hand, was a collective project of a rebellious people. They all contributed a little bit from themselves to have the metal shaped by human hands. The paleo-aesthetics of God have been abandoned yet again for slicker technology.

Their rebellion is twofold: they have rebelled against God and Moses. They have commissioned Aaron to fashion a leader for them, declaring Moses' leadership to have suffered a form of death *in absentia*. The two tiers of leadership are replaced with one idol. The calf will not only replace Yahweh, but it will replace Moses as well:

> For they said to me, "Make us gods who shall go before us. As for this Moses, the man who brought us up out of the land of Egypt, we do not know what has become of him." (Exod 32:23)

The people, in their repugnant worship of the trinket they have fashioned, declare that it is the one who has led them out of Egypt. In saying this, they prove Moses' authority yet again, for they rebel against Moses, the one who representatively led them out of Egypt, and God, who ultimately led them out of Egypt.

The contrast does not end there. Moses is given the Law to bring down the mountain and covenantally assign it to the people. The Law will tell the people exactly what God requires them to do and what not to do. Sexual immorality and greed will be front and center in that list. And yet, here is the golden calf, a fertility god made of gold, that represents the desire of the people for sex and money. Even more can be said about the kind of god their desire creates.

Ellul and Fernand Ryser both emphasize the exchange that is taking place here:

> The calf will be made with gold from the "rings that adorn the ears"; that is, which honor the organ that allows us to hear the word! "Aaron dishonors the ear; it no longer counts; now just the eye matters. Hearing the Word of God no longer matters; now seeing and looking at an image are central. Sight replaces faith. The concept that arises from a person's heart or mind is transformed into a work fashioned by human hands and takes the place of the invisible revelation that comes from above."[1]

The problem the rebels have with God is that he is not seen. The problem the rebels have with Moses is that he is not seen. They build a god they can see. This will set the stage for the future of all rejection of the Word of God. It was, in Israel's case, and has been with every unbeliever since then, an exchange of one sensory gate for another. Both hearing and seeing come from God; however, the Bible is replete with warnings about the trickery of the eye, and commands about the importance of hearing and understanding. Scripture tells us that, with God, faith comes by hearing, and hearing by the word of God (Rom 10:17). The cultures that fashion golden calves repeat the mantra that *seeing is believing*. One thinks of the tragic words often attributed to Bertrand Russell when asked what he would say to God, should he ever stand before him: "Sir, why did you take such pains to hide yourself?"

The tablets, which Moses received, were written with the finger of God. Some people have argued that this is mere anthropomorphism. They suggest that because God is a Spirit, he does not literally have a finger. Too much is lost in this attempt to rescue God from the literalists. Whatever the Spirit means by saying that God had hewn one set of stones and Moses had hewn the other must be something quite close to what it sounds like. How did God hew the stone? No one knows. Rest assured, it was different than the manner in which Moses did it. It is equally as certain that, if Moses had been commissioned to write out the Law, he would not have used his finger.

So what can be said concerning Jesus and this issuing of the Law on tablets of stone, written by the finger of God? Much. The Law is a shadow of Christ himself. Outwardly, the God of Israel is praised as the Rock. The

---

1. Ellul, *The Humiliation of the Word*, 87.

Law is Stone of Stone. The Law is the definition of the character of God. He who has seen the Son has seen the Father (John 14:9). The Law is the standard of righteousness, according to God. Christ is our righteousness, if we are in him (Rom 3:21, 1 Cor 1:30). The Law is the word of God. Christ is given the appellation "Word of God." Christ fulfilled the Law, and in the New Covenant, his governing presence is called the "Law of Christ" (Gal 6:2, 1 Cor 9:21).

In many ways, the giving of the Law can almost be seen as a shadow of a Christian creed. It shouldn't surprise us if someday we learn that the tablets of the Law on stone were an Old Testament model of the regenerate human heart. When the New Covenant was issued, the model sprang to life. It was as if the Old Testament adherent to the Law who was once cold and clunky became a real live boy. It is a kind of retelling of *The Tale of Pinocchio.* Christ, who was God of gods, fulfilled the Law of God as the Word of God. He placed himself under the tablets that had crushed everyone else, and he breathed life into them. The believer is not under the tablets of stone any longer. Because of Jesus, they can feed on the very lifestream of the character of God: his Word, his Image, his Son. The New Covenant believer does not have the Law of God written on stone; they have the Law written on atria and ventricles.

We from the Law to Christ have Turned

(Ira Sankey, 1908)

We from the law to Christ have turned;
To trust in Him by grace we've learned.
And since His glory we've discerned
We only care for Christ!

Chapter 8

And the Lord said, "Behold, there is a place by me where you shall stand on the rock, and while my glory passes by I will put you in a cleft of the rock, and I will cover you with my hand until I have passed by. Then I will take away my hand, and you shall see my back, but my face shall not be seen." (Exod 33:21–23)

BY WAY OF REMINDER, when looking for the food of the gospel anywhere in Scripture, but especially in the Old Testament, it is crucial to establish a network of related verses that communicate back and forth across covenantal lines. The best hermeneutical system is the one that emerges from the text of Scripture, like an implicit message rising to the fore of a code as it's broken.

Moses has petitioned God to abide with his people. He has requested that God be Emmanuel. He is given far more than he could possibly understand at the time. There is no doubt that these events must be surging through the redeemed mind of Moses as he would later interact with Christ on the Mount of Transfiguration. Here, suffice to say that Moses begs God for more of himself, and he is given the shadow of the cross.

God has given his Law to Israel, and has commanded them to move on from this region. Based on their behavior, thus far, he requires that they divest themselves of all their jewelry. Clearly, God knows just how deep the deceitfulness of their souls runs. No doubt, as soon as Moses turns his back again, they will be melting their necklaces down and crafting themselves images to worship. It is apparent that their desire is for a god they can see, rather than the true, but invisible, God.

As the command to leave Sinai is given, God informs Moses that he will not be joining them in as intimate a fashion as would have been hoped for by by this expatriate of Egypt. The Lord informs him that his position regarding the people is one of being on the edge of consuming them. They are rebellious and hidebound. They can't be trusted to carry their own trinkets. God will not commit to traveling in the midst of such a group.

Curiously, Moses exhibits a deeply ingrained advocacy for this people who can't seem to ever defy him enough. This must not be attributed to any inherent grace on Moses' part. He himself is a grumbler and rebel. He advocates for Israel because he is a type of Christ, and a self-professing forerunner of the Redeemer (Deut 18). He advocates for Israel because he has been called to the task of intercession by God himself. Without reducing this complexity to insanity, it must be understood that it is God in Moses interceding for the people of God. There is no grace that finds its origin in Miriam's brother, which is to be seen in opposition to the grace of God. There must be an allowance for a complexity of plot that corresponds in magnitude to God being the protagonist. Moses is commissioned by God to play the part of God's representative:

> God also said to Moses, "Say this to the people of Israel: 'The Lord, the God of your fathers, the God of Abraham, the God of Isaac, and the God of Jacob, has sent me to you.'" (Exod 3:15a)

Finally, after a beautiful interaction in which Moses pleads with God on behalf of sinners, God appears to draw out of Moses the theological concept he had hidden in the argument all along. Moses appeals to the presence of God amongst his people as the only defining characteristic that separates them from every other group of pagans on planet Earth. Without the presence of God in their midst, there is no people of God. At this, God seems satisfied. Moses has preached properly. God will join his people. Then, reminiscent of Abraham, when he dared to ask God for one more thing, Moses boldly refuses to be satisfied with his present relationship with God if there is more to be had. After asking God to give himself to sinners, and most likely bolstered by God's response of being pleased with Moses and his name being known by God, he implores the Lord to show him his glory.

Because the Creator God is not an idol, he cannot be seen. Not wanting to leave Moses' prayer for more of him unanswered, God tells Moses that there is something he will do for him. God tells his friend that he will place him upon the rock, and allow his glory to be experienced in a visible way, in the only way possible.

A quick reading of the text will possibly cause one to miss the first and most important answer to Moses' prayer. He asks God for a vision of his glory, and God responds by a guarantee of being near him.

And the Lord said, "Behold, there is a place by me." (Exod 33:21a)

Keeping in mind the Pauline promise that the history of Israel is actually a historically true allegory which was recorded for the instruction of New Covenant believers (1 Cor 10:11), one should expect to find the gospel of Jesus in more accounts than merely the Rock at Horeb (1 Cor 10:4). It cannot be overstated that if one were to begin with the Old Testament, they would not find the gospel in these passages, for it is concealed. Because the gospel is revealed in the New Testament, one is able to read the Bible from right to left and see the gospel in the Old Testament, because of the interpretive lens of the New Testament.

Moses asked to see God's glory, and he was seated with God in a heavenly place. The leader of Israel is placed near God, in order to see what can be seen of an unseen God. This is crucial. When dealing with the Creator God, there is no vantage point by which we can accurately assess him, apart from being close to him. This why the scoffing and mocking of hecklers will be silenced—they know him not.

Continuing to understand God's good news, through his own use of the rock and stone motif, one begins to see the overwhelming answer to Moses' request for more of God. It is an inspiration to approach the throne boldly. It is an encouraging word for those who dare not be satisfied with one's present sounding in the fathomless God. Press into him. He will give more. Remember the lesson that God taught Ezekiel:

> Going on eastward with a measuring line in his hand, the man measured a thousand cubits, and then led me through the water, and it was ankle-deep. Again he measured a thousand, and led me through the water, and it was knee-deep. Again he measured a thousand, and led me through the water, and it was waist-deep. Again he measured a thousand, and it was a river that I could not pass through, for the water had risen. It was deep enough to swim in, a river that could not be passed through. (Ezek 47:3–5)

What is it that Moses sees? He is shown what a man can see of God and still live. He sees a visible representation of the Unseen God. In the New Testament, the only thing that matches this description is Christ himself. He is the Image of the invisible God (Col 1:15). He is the only One with whom God will share his glory (Isa 42:8, Matt 16:27, John 17:5).

In chapter 5, it was shown how Moses was positioned in the posture of the Father God, by being poised upon the rock; but his posture becomes more Christlike when we realize that his arms are outstretched. His posture becomes even more Christlike when we are told by Paul that the Rock was Jesus. The Rock was smitten, stricken, and afflicted. The people drank from its wounded side.

There is, in this passage, an allegorical positioning of Moses in the seat of Christ. He is on the rock and in the Rock. If we were to say this of Christ, the creedal language would be that of John 1. He was with God, and was God. This image is also true for those who are said to be "in God." They are hemmed in on all sides by the will of the Lord. When the people of God are "in God," though they cannot see him with sight, they behold him by faith, and this faith comes by hearing his word. This faith-based and Scripture-based vision is so superior that it inspires the rejection of false gods—just what these idolaters need:

> And your ears shall hear a word behind you, saying, "This is the way, walk in it," when you turn to the right or when you turn to the left. Then you will defile your carved idols overlaid with silver and your gold-plated metal images. You will scatter them as unclean things. You will say to them, "Be gone!" (Isa 30:21–22)

Who is being hidden from the wind in the shade of a great rock in a weary land? It is Moses. Who is the stammerer who finds his voice in the service of the righteous King? It is Moses. Who experiences the reality of streams of water in a dry place? It is Moses. But these things are not nearly as true in a Mosaic fulfillment as they are when ultimately fulfilled by Christ. Moses sits in the seat of Christ during a time when the gospel is concealed. Now that we know what the gospel "looks like," it is more easily recognized in its natural habitat:

> Behold, a king will reign in righteousness, and princes will rule in justice. Each will be like a hiding place from the wind, a shelter from the storm, like streams of water in a dry place, like the shade of a great rock in a weary land. Then the eyes of those who see will not be closed, and the ears of those who hear will give attention. The heart of the hasty will understand and know, and the tongue of the stammerers will hasten to speak distinctly. (Isa 32:1–4)

The presence of the Rock functions as mediation for this mediator. It is the liaison that allows a holy God and sinful man to interface in a manner that should not be possible. In this way, the Rock is Christ. Remember, the Rock is with God, because the position given to Moses is "by [God]."

Then I will take away my hand, and you shall see my back, but my face shall not be seen. (Exod 33:23)

Here, the removal of God's hand and his back being turned are both gestures which have been historically represented as the judgment of God. Sometimes God extends his hand in regards to sin, and sometimes he removes his hand of protection. Sometimes he sees the sin and does not turn his face away, and sometimes he turns his back on people because of their sin. In this case, it is appropriate to think of Moses as sitting in the seat of Christ, allegorically, and catching a glimpse from the view of the cross. In other words, in order to view God properly, one must be positioned with Christ—the one whom experienced God turning his back and removing his hand. In order to see God, we must see Christ.

He has cut down in fierce anger all the might of Israel; he has withdrawn from them his right hand in the face of the enemy; he has burned like a flaming fire in Jacob, consuming all around. (Lam 2:3)

But your iniquities have made a separation between you and your God, and your sins have hidden his face from you so that he does not hear. (Isa 59:2)

For you have died, and your life is hidden with Christ in God. (Col 3:3)

Christ's agony is seen is the removal of the Father's hand, and the turning away of his face. The beauty of the gospel, rightly understood and experienced by Moses, is that this scene is actually beautiful. It is an answer to the prayer that Moses might see the glory of God. There is no other place to see this glory more fully than in the person and work of Jesus. The horror of Calvary's agony must be precious in the eyes of the believer. It must be the inciter of worship. It is for this reason that A. W. Tozer's full quote, previously referenced, reads as follows:

We must hide our unholiness in the wounds of Christ as Moses hid himself in the cleft of the rock while the glory of God passed by. We must take refuge from God in God. Above all we must believe that God sees us perfect in His Son while He disciplines and chastens and purges us that we may be partakers of His holiness.[1]

---

1. Tozer, *The Knowledge of the Holy*, 107.

The prayer of Moses is being answered in a way that Moses could not have then understood. He desired to see the glory of God, and he was given a view of God from the vantage point of the cross. He asked for the glory of the Father, and he was placed in the bosom of the Beloved. He sought after the presence of God, on behalf of himself and the elect, and he was given Emmanuel.

He Hideth my Soul

(Fanny Crosby, 1890)

A wonderful Savior is Jesus my Lord,
A wonderful Savior to me;
He hideth my soul in the cleft of the rock,
Where rivers of pleasure I see.

He hideth my soul in the cleft of the rock,
That shadows a dry, thirsty land;
He hideth my life in the depths of His love,
And covers me there with His hand,
And covers me there with His hand.

Chapter 9

And Moses lifted up his hand and struck the rock with his staff twice, and water came out abundantly, and the congregation drank, and their livestock. And the Lord said to Moses and Aaron, "Because you did not believe in me, to uphold me as holy in the eyes of the people of Israel, therefore you shall not bring this assembly into the land that I have given them." (Num 20:11–12)

THERE IS A STRONG pull that many people experience, toward ways of ministering the gospel that depend upon great pomp and spectacle. It sometimes seems that plain old preaching is pedestrian, when compared with film clips, dramatic productions, incense, or Latin homilies.

When my wife and I were in college, in the Bible Belt, there was a church in our town that was notorious for its employment of spectacle. Some of our friends returned from service one morning turbo-charged over the newest strain of creativity that had infected the church. As the pastor was about to make his way to the pulpit, the lights began to flicker and then move on and off in a swirling pattern throughout the building. The drums began to roll like thunder and an announcer's voice came out of the fog, straining to keep himself from losing control. He bellowed with the windup of a television wrestling emcee, "Heeeeeeeeeerre's Paaaaaaaaaaaastor Rooooooooooooooobbieeeeeeeeeeeeeee!!" At the same time, the worship band exploded into a brilliant (but designer impostor) version of one of AC/DC's most famous opening riffs, and in came the pastor, blasting through the front doors on his newest model of Harley Davidson motorcycle, down the center aisle and onto the stage via a specially constructed ramp. "How attractive Christianity was made to be," pondered my friends aloud, "to that crowd of visitors who raised their hands at the end of the service."

Hearken back to the passage in Exodus 17 in which Moses and Aaron beseech God as to what to do about the restless crowds. The people of Israel began to grumble against the divinely appointed leadership, all on account of their being thirsty. Upon inquiry, Moses is told that God would place his presence on the Rock at Horeb, in this region which would heretofore be called Massah and Meribah. With God positioned on the Rock, the Rock was to be struck with the staff. Water would flow from the Rock and the thirsty people would drink. Moses obeyed, and sinners drank from the Rock which was struck for them. This Rock, we are told by Paul, was Christ.

> For I do not want you to be unaware, brothers, that our fathers were all under the cloud, and all passed through the sea, and all were baptized into Moses in the cloud and in the sea, and all ate the same spiritual food, and all drank the same spiritual drink. For they drank from the spiritual Rock that followed them, and the Rock was Christ. (1 Cor 10:1–4)

Thirty-nine years later, we see in Numbers 20 a very familiar situation. Some have inquired as to why this "water from the rock" scenario is so remarkably similar to the first. In both events, the people are thirsty. In both events, Moses and Aaron inquire of God. In both events, God tells Moses to take his staff and approach the Rock. In both events, God says he will give them water from the Rock, and the people will drink. It is the very same region. The parts overlap. As far as we know, it is the exact same Rock. Why? Our answer comes from Paul, "For they drank from the spiritual Rock that followed them, and the Rock was Christ."

The fact that Israel is wandering in circles is not the reason for arriving a second time at Horeb. Well, it's a very good reason, but only in a secondary fashion. We have been told that they were not following this Rock; on the contrary, this Rock was following them. That is not to say that the Rock had moved. It is that there was a meaning to this Rock and meaning to the event of their thirst being slaked from this Rock that would be central to their identity. At the beginning and end of their wanderings, they engage this Rock for water. It is not that they have decided to return to their starting point. It is not that, as chance would have it, they passed by this place twice. No. It is a lesson on election. The Rock was following them. The Rock would give them his sustenance based on his choosing, and his electing them, not the other way around.

Imagine a family on vacation, presumably lost and driving in circles through a national park. Hours after passing it the first time, a child in the back seat notices a historic monument and remarks, "I think I know this monument." By way of analogy, Paul would tell us that at this point, the monument opens his mouth and says, "I've known you since before the foundations of the world." This is not a stretch. This is exactly what is taught in Scripture. They did not circle back in their wanderings to the Rock at which they'd started; the Rock marked them out as his own and brought them home.

It will become more relevant as this passage unfolds, but it must be noted that this second event of the water in the Rock is stationed between the death of Miriam and the death of Aaron. It will be the death sentence for Moses as well, but he does not know this going into it.

The pointed difference between the two events in question is that, in the first session, Moses was commanded to strike the Rock that was housing the presence of God. It is not redundant to restate that the Scriptures tell us this Rock was Jesus. In the second instance, Moses was specifically told to speak to the Rock, and water would issue forth. What could this possibly mean?

As with the entire text of the Bible, it is necessary to take what we know of Scripture and begin to graph the basic structure of hermeneutical understanding by using pertinent Scriptures as the boundaries, within which we can expect to locate the gospel meaning. In this case, we are given an enormous help by Paul, under the inspiration of the Holy Spirit, telling us that the Rock is Christ.

If there were a flannelgraph board installed at the front of the room, one can imagine that a figure of Moses could be stuck to the left side, frantically wielding a stick over his head, with which we are to imagine that he has struck the gray bolder that clings to the right side of the flannelgraph. A jet of water bursts like a whale's spout from the side of the gray rock. While keeping this scenario in your mind, peel off the gray rock and put up the image of Christ on the cross. Now we see the whale spout of water issuing forth from his pierced side. Now we see Moses, in a prophetic and priestly fashion, striking the Savior on behalf of the sinful masses.

The flannelgraph schema of Horeb actually portrays the typological weight of the situation in a manner that is helpful. To be able to peel off the Rock and insert the more antitypical crucified Lord allows the rest of the math to graph out beautifully around it.

In the first scene, Christ is crucified. The presence of God is placed on the Rock, and the Rock is struck. Water issues forth from his side, and all the people drink and are satisfied. God's presence dwells on the Rock in such a way that Moses must confront the heavy truth that it is God himself whom he is striking. As if that weren't enough, this trepidatious act is done on behalf of rebellious sinners. Amen.

In the second scene, the props are all familiar, and the plot is similar because Jesus is following them. They are part of a history that is taking place in order to be understood allegorically, and is being written down for the sake of New Covenant believers who will have the fully revealed gospel in their minds as they read it. I've mentioned it in previous chapters, but here again the words of Paul:

> Now these things happened to them as an example, but they were written down for our instruction, on whom the end of the ages has come. (1 Cor 10:11)

Moses is commanded to speak to the Rock, in order that water might flow from it. Why is this an important distinction? Because two things are taking place: the primacy of shepherding is being given to preaching, and the re-presentation of the sacrifice of Christ is condemned as being irreverent.

Notice that striking the Rock is the one thing that is swapped out. Everything else is very similar. Moses is commanded to speak, not strike. This happens because the event being typified in the first encounter at Horeb is the crucifixion and it is sufficient once, and only once. If there was any room for a re-presentation of the crucifixion, this would be the place. Moses is not literally crucifying Christ; he is offering allegorical representations of it. This is besides the point. The power of the crucifixion is that it is effectively done once, and any remembrance of it must be distinguished from re-presentations of it. This cannot be overstated. It was the re-presentation of the crucifixion that got Moses killed. God calls it blasphemy and issues a sober and final sentence upon a man whom he called from birth, and has spent many years in faithful ministry.

So, why does God go so far as to say that Moses' great crime in his action was that he was unbelieving, and did not regard God as holy? This is the case because it is the crucifixion of his Son that is in God's mind when it is taking place the first time. Remember, according to Paul's criterion, it is the crucifixion of Christ that should be in our minds when we read this as well.

> And the Lord said to Moses and Aaron, "Because you did not believe in me, to uphold me as holy in the eyes of the people of Israel, therefore you shall not bring this assembly into the land that I have given them." (Num 20:12)

Once the striking of the Rock was established, once and for all, the work that would follow would be the proclaiming of the Word of God. This is being portrayed as the work God requires on top of the foundation of Christ's finished work. In our day, we call this preaching. Even the writer of Hebrews, when beginning a section of Scripture on the once and for all nature of the work of Christ on the cross, moves through a discourse that arrives at the present end, which he describes as a confessing body of believers. It is a movement from the crucifixion to the proclaimed word.

> And by that will we have been sanctified through the offering of the body of Jesus Christ once for all. And every priest stands daily at his service, offering repeatedly the same sacrifices, which can never take away sins. But when Christ had offered for all time a single sacrifice for sins, he sat down at the right hand of God, waiting from that time until his enemies should be made a footstool for his feet. For by a single offering he has perfected for all time those who are being sanctified. And the Holy Spirit also bears witness to us; for after saying, "This is the covenant that I will make with them after those days, declares the Lord: I will put my laws on their hearts, and write them on their minds," then he adds, "I will remember their sins and their lawless deeds no more." Where there is forgiveness of these, there is no longer any offering for sin. Therefore, brothers, since we have confidence to enter the holy places by the blood of Jesus, by the new and living way that he opened for us through the curtain, that is, through his flesh, and since we have a great priest over the house of God, let us draw near with a true heart in full assurance of faith, with our hearts sprinkled clean from an evil conscience and our bodies washed with pure water. Let us hold fast the confession of our hope without wavering, for he who promised is faithful. (Heb 10:10–23)

An obvious note that needs addressing is the inevitable outpouring of water that still issued forth, despite Moses' irreverence. Clearly, there is no confusion over whether or not Moses' actions were right or sinful. That is not a thing that is determined by resulting fruit. How many men of God have justified their secret sins, thinking them passed over by God, because of the ensuing fruit that God brought forth through them. Time after time, this thinking proves to be tragic. God does not change. He despises sin, and will not tolerate it. That is not to say he cannot work in spite of it.

Water came out from the rock because of God's actions, not Moses'. There is no exception to this in all of church history. There is no man or woman, boy or girl, who has seen fruit come from their striving, who can take even the smallest amount of credit. All they did was their job. Sometimes that is done well and sometimes that is done poorly. There is no flat superimposition of God only bringing fruit about at the hands of flawless vessels. On the contrary. Christ being preached through selfish ambition, at best, only preaches Christ; it in no way sanctifies selfish ambition:

> Some indeed preach Christ from envy and rivalry, but others from good will. The latter do it out of love, knowing that I am put here for the defense of the gospel. The former proclaim Christ out of selfish ambition, not sincerely but thinking to afflict me in my imprisonment. What then? Only that in every way, whether in pretense or in truth, Christ is proclaimed, and in that I rejoice. (Phil 1:15–18)

Two things should be said about Moses' death sentence. Some will, undoubtedly, recoil at the thought that such a seemingly nuanced infraction rendered Moses unfit to enter the Promised Land, and even rendered it necessary for him to die. In light of the fact that God is God and he changeth not, this passage could be the cause of fear and trembling. That may be a good thing; nevertheless, it must be said that this passage, like all of Scripture, is designed to preach the gospel. Even the Law, if used properly, should bring someone to the cross of Christ and not merely one's own tombstone. God is still the same holy God who cannot abide even the slightest infraction; but the judgment is not left to be weighed on the scales of our cumulative actions. We are not hoping for our good to outweigh our bad. One small instruction left unfollowed meant immediate death for someone who is called "a friend of God." If this is true, what hope is there for sinners who are far worse? Much, indeed. Christ was ultimately crucified for the sins of all those who trust in him, so that they need not be destroyed for their own sin. This includes Moses. Moses entered the ultimate Promised Land, though the inferior one was kept from him. He did not enter based on his merit, but the merit of the One in whom he trusted, whom he preached, and whom he crucified with his own sins.

The second thing is this: Jesus gave his people the prayer often called "The Lord's Prayer," because it is a corrective tool. We go to this prayer to learn how to pray the way Jesus prayed. We do not intuitively know how to pray. We come to God with requests for our kingdoms to be advanced and our wills to be done. We write out these requests under the heading "Prayer List." Jesus reforms our prayerful inclination, and remakes it around that which is right—namely, the will of God. The reverence of God is the corrective to Moses' sin for which we are to daily pray. "Hallowed be Thy Name" means "Let your Name be treated carefully and respectfully as I now fearfully use it." It is the couplet concept to our praying "in Jesus' name." Had Moses prayed like this, prior to his entering into the second event at Horeb, perhaps the story would be different.

God is holy and must be revered as being holy. But the cross of Christ is the liaison between sinful humans and a holy God. To be found in Christ is to be reconciled to a holy God, made righteous, and yet know that one is, simultaneously, the worst sinner in the room. Christ was crucified once and for all, the righteous for the unrighteous. The work of the church, in light of this foundation having already been laid, is to faithfully proclaim the Word of God. This is the vehicle God has ordained for the distribution of faith. What might be different in the imprint of redemptive history, had Moses preached the word instead of offering the Mass? We can't say. But we can learn from his example, which was written down for our sake, upon whom the ends of the ages have come.

The Second Striking of the Rock in the Desert

Hymn #163
(Spooner, Thomas, E. Dilly, *300 Hymns*, London, 1762)

As in the fortieth year again,
The Jews for water cry
With murmurs; so the Church at times
Falls by Iniquity.

Their leader strikes a Rock again,
Without Divine command.
Fors Jesus was but once to die
By persecuting hand.

Chapter 10

Give ear, O heavens, and I will speak, and let the earth hear the words of my mouth. May my teaching drop as the rain, my speech distill as the dew, like gentle rain upon the tender grass, and like showers upon the herb. For I will proclaim the name of the Lord; ascribe greatness to our God! The Rock, his work is perfect, for all his ways are justice. A God of faithfulness and without iniquity, just and upright is he. They have dealt corruptly with him; they are no longer his children because they are blemished; they are a crooked and twisted generation . . . You were unmindful of the Rock that bore you, and you forgot the God who gave you birth . . . If they were wise, they would understand this; they would discern their latter end! How could one have chased a thousand, and two have put ten thousand to flight unless their Rock had sold them, and the Lord had given them up? For their rock is not as our Rock; our enemies are by themselves. (Deut 32:1–5, 18, 29–31)

GOD WROTE A SONG about a rock. He said his lyrics were like raindrops. It's a kids' song. At the beginning of it, he commanded that the whole universe had to listen to it. What a song. There is a bird in it. There is a part where rocks that aren't really rocks convince some kids to hate their family so much that they run away. Many of them became enemies of their Father and a war ensues. When the Rock finally finishes the war, the whole universe claps its hands, and kids from every generation end up singing God's song, over and over.

After turning one hundred twenty, Moses faces the sober reality that his race is coming to an end. He has had some time to deal with the reality that his last course of events at Meribah have left a certain kind of blemish on his legacy. This is a man who, on a few occasions, allowed anger to rule him. From his slaying of the Egyptian guard, to the breaking of the tablets of the Law, to his dishonoring the Name of the Lord at Horeb, Moses' sins are forgiven and forgotten as far as he is concerned, but they were written down for our sake, upon whom the ends of the ages have come. A man with a recurring sin pattern may be forgiven, but he will live and die outside the gate of a joy and peace he might have known.

The mantle has been passed off to Joshua and, in prophetic fashion, Joshua leads God's people into their rest. Moses' final work, before leaving office, was to record this song and recite it to Israel. It is a song that God himself wrote. It is a kind of time capsule. God knows that the people will rebel against him. He has them memorize it, and each generation sing it, so that when the people do rebel against God, and they will, the children of that generation will sing its words in the street and the air will ring with the indictment of God against a corrupt and twisted generation who ran away from the Rock.

> "Now therefore write this song and teach it to the people of Israel. Put it in their mouths, that this song may be a witness for me against the people of Israel. For when I have brought them into the land flowing with milk and honey, which I swore to give to their fathers, and they have eaten and are full and grown fat, they will turn to other gods and serve them, and despise me and break my covenant. And when many evils and troubles have come upon them, this song shall confront them as a witness (for it will live unforgotten in the mouths of their offspring). For I know what they are inclined to do even today, before I have brought them into the land that I swore to give." So Moses wrote this song the same day and taught it to the people of Israel. (Deut 31:19–22)

In some camps, the doctrine of the impassibility of God is presented in such a fashion as to render him heartless, literally. Even in those extremes, however, the impulse that defines God as being without passions is often well-meaning and, in some ways, sound. The Westminster Confession of Faith defines the doctrine of divine impassibility as follows:

> There is but one only, living, and true God, who is infinite in being and perfection, a most pure spirit, invisible, without body, parts, or passions; immutable, immense, eternal, incomprehensible, almighty, most wise, most holy, most free, most absolute; working all things according to the counsel of His own immutable and most righteous will, for His own glory; most loving, gracious, merciful, long-suffering, abundant in goodness and truth, forgiving iniquity, transgression, and sin; the rewarder of them that diligently

seek Him; and withal, most just, and terrible in His judgments, hating all sin, and who will by no means clear the guilty.[1]

Some argue that impassibility developed over time as a necessary counter-response to an attack on the immutability of God.[2] In our day, it is regularly and understandably leveled against the popular heresy of open theism. There are important qualifiers which must be employed in a conversation about God and whether he experiences emotion or not. Even the Westminster holds God as without passions in the same paragraph that states He is most loving and that He hates all sin. Clearly, zero emotion must not be the target. It is helpful to see the manner in which God introduces himself as the Rock in Deuteronomy 32.

> The Rock, his work is perfect, for all his ways are justice. A God of faithfulness and without iniquity, just and upright is he. They have dealt corruptly with him; they are no longer his children because they are blemished; they are a crooked and twisted generation. You were unmindful of the Rock that bore you, and you forgot the God who gave you birth. (Deut 32:4–6)

When we examine the Levitical descriptions of what true justice looks like, it is consistently described as right judgment that is not drawn aside by emotional influence (Exod 23:3, Lev 19:15). The Rock is perfect, and every one of his inclinations is just. He has no fault. There is no soft spot in him, by which iniquity could gain a foothold; nor the slightest breach through which righteousness might be depleted. This is an important fact to remember in relation to the cross. The cross of Christ is not only the greatest act of charity in the history of the cosmos, it is the greatest moment of justice ever conceived by the legal mind. God does not wink at sin. He does not overlook iniquity. It must be dealt with, and properly. It must be dealt with in such a manner that it is not tampered with, in any way, by faintness of heart or personal investment. In this way, the cross of Christ is only possible if God the Father is impassible. His relationship with the Son is one that includes pleasure and love. He has told us so. Because perfect justice on a human's behalf could only be required at the hands of a man who was also God, the Father had to be impassible—not simply for a moment, but in substance. And when the impassible God performed the purest act of justice, without being tempered by any fit of emotional

---

1. Schaff, *The Creeds of Christendom*, 3.606.
2. Grudem, *Systematic Theology*, 163.

attachment, he stood back and said, "Now that is perfect love" (John 3:16). If anyone ever doubted whether the Creator God was emotive, perfect justice answers it resoundingly: *Yes!* Impassibility is only half the story. It's the half that is necessary for us to understand what God means when he says, non-anthropomorphically, that he loved the world so much.

It is for this reason—the stability of a God who references himself as the Rock—that the rebelliousness of unbelieving Israel is described as crooked and twisted. What can be manipulated into such distorted adjectives? Not rock. All sin is injustice, as any decent catechism will tell you, because it is transgressing the Law of God. That is why David repents to God after committing murder and adultery with human beings (Ps 51:4). It is why Paul can say that greed and covetousness are acts of idolatry, because it is an act of unbelief against the God who has supplied all your needs, according to his riches in glory (Col 3:5, Phil 4:19). Twistedness is a way to describe things that move and are prone to deviation. This is not the rock. His stability is sure. All deviation is measured against his stability.

This Deuteronomy passage does not, however, merely describe God as an unflinching Judge. In his study entitled *Sonship*, Jack Miller, under much criticism from his contemporaries, dares to conflate some aspects of justification and adoption by suggesting that the Judge does not merely pound the gavel and say, "You're free to go." Not at all. He pounds the gavel and says, "You're free to go . . . you're free to go home with me, son."[3]

The Judge does not merely reference himself as the Rock, but he also references himself as the Father of Children. Were it not for the case that Scripture plainly speaks of the children of God as living stones, one might be tempted to suggest that the metaphoric vehicle was failing to accomplish its purpose. But it is not. This Rock has children by faith, and they are born of his Spirit. The difference between them and the Son by Whom all others enter the family is the difference between being begotten and adopted. It is only confusing because the adoption process is spiritual birth. The begotten of the Father is the Chief Cornerstone. He is a Rock like the Father:

> Built on the foundation of the apostles and prophets, Christ Jesus himself being the cornerstone. (Eph 2:20)

God, the Rock, is the Father of his people. They exist in the same antinome that surrounds him: the Rock is alive. The stones that are joined into him are born of him. They are living stones, and they have come from him.

3. Miller, *Sonship*, 52.

> You yourselves like living stones are being built up as a spiritual
> house, to be a holy priesthood, to offer spiritual sacrifices accept-
> able to God through Jesus Christ. (1 Pet 2:5)

To have the Rock as Father is to have an indomitable defense. To have the Rock in any way is to be protected on all sides, as when Moses was hid in its cleft. No one else has this kind of defense. When the people lose the presence of the Rock, it plays out in space/time reality as them being possessed or attacked by another nation. This should not be the case, because their rock is not a true rock. There is only one Rock. Nevertheless, to wander from God is to wander from the safety of home. Obedience and submission to the authority of God actually produce freedom. To rebel is to find out what it is to be isolated prey.

It is not only in his fatherly description of himself as the Rock of Defense that God declares his loving kindness and protection of his people. In the middle of the song of God, he describes himself as a mama bird. This is a practice to which Jesus is drawn as well (Matt 23:37). In the Deuteronomy passage, God not only dons the simile of a mother bird, but one who can remarkably feed his young with honey and oil that issue from the Rock.

> Like an eagle that stirs up its nest, that flutters over its young,
> spreading out its wings, catching them, bearing them on its pin-
> ions, the Lord alone guided him, no foreign god was with him.
> He made him ride on the high places of the land, and he ate the
> produce of the field, and he suckled him with honey out of the
> rock, and oil out of the flinty rock. (Deut 32:11–13)

There is a resounding tale in this passage, whose dark moral rings through the ages and into our own day: to be without God is to experience perpetual fatherlessness. The only God that exists is the one with all the kids. There are a million and one ways to be alone. It is not possible with God. "For their rock is not as our Rock; our enemies are by themselves."

The layers of counter-intuitive symbolism are staggering. God does not only sing about himself being the Rock, but the Rock who had children. He is not only the Rock who had children, but he is One that is like a mother eagle. He is not like any mother eagle, but One that feeds with honey and oil from the Rock. He is the only defense, and the only stable, unshifting shelter in a world full of snakes. He is the Rock, and those who are in him are of him and are like him. Those who are in him shall not be moved.

Under His Wings

(William Orcutt Cushing, 1870)

Under His wings I am safely abiding;
Though the night deepens and tempests are wild,
Still I can trust Him, I know He will keep me;
He has redeemed me, and I am His child.
Under His wings, under His wings,
Who from His love can sever?
Under His wings my soul shall abide,
Safely abide forever.

Under His wings—what a refuge in sorrow!
How the heart yearningly turns to His rest!
Often when earth has no balm for my healing,
There I find comfort, and there I am blest.

Under His wings—oh, what precious enjoyment!
There will I hide till life's trials are o'er;
Sheltered, protected, no evil can harm me;
Resting in Jesus I'm safe evermore.

Chapter 11

So Joshua made a covenant with the people that day, and put in place statutes and rules for them at Shechem. And Joshua wrote these words in the Book of the Law of God. And he took a large stone and set it up there under the terebinth that was by the sanctuary of the Lord. And Joshua said to all the people, "Behold, this stone shall be a witness against us, for it has heard all the words of the Lord that he spoke to us. Therefore it shall be a witness against you, lest you deal falsely with your God." So Joshua sent the people away, every man to his inheritance. (Josh 24:25–28)

COMPARED WITH THE AMOUNT of Scripture that centers on the dealings of God with Moses, Joshua seems to assume leadership and arrive at his own death fairly quickly. In this passage, at the end of the book of Joshua, he is preparing to die. His life has been a full one. He has seen Rahab hide his two spies, thereby aiding the Israelites in taking the city of Jericho. He has seen God hold the sun still in the sky. He has successfully brought the people of God into the promised land, and this without the company of Moses.

This is the generation of children who have become adults in the context of nomadic wanderings. Although the promise of a home has been constantly in front of them, guaranteed by the word of God, in every practical sense, they have been homeless. Because of their unbelief and rebellion, almost all of their parents were assigned to death in the wilderness. Now, Joshua is sending them out to their allotted inheritance.

It's impossible for Joshua to ignore the prophetic warning that, as soon as these people have unpacked, they will begin to rebel against God. The song of God which Moses taught them, the warnings of the Law and the Covenant, and now Joshua himself, all attest to the fact that their inclination is away from the Lord. Knowing this, Joshua sets himself like flint against the tide of popular opinion. It is in this chapter he famously states that, regardless of where everyone else is headed, as for him and his family, they will serve the Lord.

> Now therefore fear the Lord and serve him in sincerity and in faithfulness. Put away the gods that your fathers served beyond the River and in Egypt, and serve the Lord. And if it is evil in your eyes to serve the Lord, choose this day whom you will serve, whether the gods your fathers served in the region beyond the River, or the gods of the Amorites in whose land you dwell. But as for me and my house, we will serve the Lord. (Josh 24:14–15)

But Joshua is dying, and the responsibility of the man of God lies not merely with those of his own day. The spiritual man is to contribute a God-ward legacy to the metanarrative of his community's future. Moses knew it. He appointed Joshua with the laying on of hands (Deut 34). He preached the Law a second time. He blessed each of the twelve tribes by name, with the love of a father who was leaving behind his boys (Deut 33). Joshua has not forgotten this rite of passage. He plans for his departure. He invests in the future of the people amongst whom he lived. He preaches one last message. He secures the giving of statutes and the covenant. He tells the people he is dying. And he erects a stone in public, next to the sanctuary.

This stone functions in a manner similar to the song of God which Moses taught to Israel: it is to be a witness against them when they begin to stray. Between the testimony of Moses, Joshua, and God himself, there is no doubt that Israel will be unfaithful. Although Joshua is leaving, and will no longer be around to personally preach a doctrine of repentance, he appoints the rock to bear witness. It has heard all of his warnings and God's commandments, and, like the song, will remain as an unflinching standard when the people stray.

Yet again, the rock ends up functioning as a representative of the authority of God. It stands as an unchanging witness, imbued with the purpose it was given in Joshua's testimony. It is inescapable. If it were possible for this story to be seen by someone outside the time-bound flow of Israel's history, it would appear as though the rock were becoming straighter and taller. This would not be because the rock is changing, but because the people are changing. They are bending and twisting away from the word of God, and, thusly, God himself.

The word of God has always functioned as a ruler by which the inclinations and conduct of people are to be judged. Christians do not ask themselves what they think about this or that issue. They ask themselves what the Bible says. In Revelation, the canon is used as the standard by which the city of God is measured. It is to be the standard of judgment for his people. This monumental rock functions in a testimonial way, not as the Law, but as an antiphonal response to the presence of the Law in their midst. If the people do not hear the Law, the rock does. The Law, inscribed on rock, is heard by the blank rock, and bears witness. Isn't that what Joshua says the role of this rock is to be? It is to be a witness of the word of the Lord that was written on stone tablets. This rock will hear the word of God and will record it in some way. "Behold, this stone shall be a witness against us, for it has heard all the words of the Lord that he spoke to us."

Deep calls out to deep. Of course it is not that the rock will literally store data; it is that the purpose of the rock, in its presence amongst the people, has been named out loud in the sanctuary. No one can look at the rock, or even pass by, without having to face the unspoken reality that God's Word stands as a stolid, fixed, and immutable center. In our day, this would be like a church that preaches the whole counsel of Scripture. It would be a church that preaches the word of God, even when the word has a sharp edge that cuts the people.

For this people to have a rock placed as a fixture near the sanctuary is deeply personal. Even if they did not see it and think of Bethel, or the altars of their forefathers, they must remember Horeb, the stone upon which Moses sat, the stone tablets of the Law, and the cleft of the rock. They must remember Joshua's purpose in erecting this stone.

Only the old timers who had lived during Joshua's day carried on the zeal and discipline of following the path laid out for them. The generation who had not known Joshua lacked a sense of connection to the Law of Moses. The edges of the tablets began to cut them when the Law was read. Of course, part of this has to do with the nature of the Sinaitic Covenant. It was never meant to be around forever. It served a purpose for a time—and it served that purpose perfectly. The fault is not to be placed on the covenant, but rather on the sinfulness of the people. That is not to suggest that, if the people had been better, the covenant would have remained. It would not have remained. It was never designed to abide:

> In speaking of a new covenant, he makes the first one obsolete. And what is becoming obsolete and growing old is ready to vanish away. (Heb 8:13)

> Now if the ministry of death, carved in letters on stone, came with such glory that the Israelites could not gaze at Moses' face because of its glory, which was being brought to an end, will not the ministry of the Spirit have even more glory? For if there was glory in the ministry of condemnation, the ministry of righteousness must far exceed it in glory. Indeed, in this case, what once had glory has come to have no glory at all, because of the glory that surpasses it. For if what was being brought to an end came with glory, much more will what is permanent have glory. (2 Cor 3:7–11)

When Joshua declares that, because it has heard the word of God, the rock will function as a witness against the people, he wants them to know he means it. It is not a riddle or a cipher. He is not hiding the meaning. The meaning exists both literally and symbolically. There is a double-helix of both spiritual and physical reality present. Here is a rock that holds great symbolic meaning. The meaning of the rock is the judgment of God. It is necessary to understand that God does not need a physical witness. If all the people should walk away from God and follow their own sinful passions, he could call to a rock, and a rock would come to bear witness against them. Throughout Scripture, we see God ready to call on lifeless stones to speak up, and he urges us to believe that they will. We have no reason to doubt the truth of it. This concept not only exists in Scripture in relation to judgment, but worship as well:

> As he was drawing near—already on the way down the Mount of Olives—the whole multitude of his disciples began to rejoice and praise God with a loud voice for all the mighty works that they had seen, saying, "Blessed is the King who comes in the name of the Lord! Peace in heaven and glory in the highest!" And some of the Pharisees in the crowd said to him, "Teacher, rebuke your disciples." He answered, "I tell you, if these were silent, the very stones would cry out." (Luke 19:37–40)

Everything in existence will glorify God. Nature already does. In the judgment, however, there will be synesthetic knowledge that is used to judge the people. Thoughts will be seen. Prayers will be smelled. Abel's blood cried out from the ground. It did not stain the ground, as one might expect blood to do. It cried out. This must not be sloughed off as hyperbole. One should expect that, in the judgement, rocks and trees and birds and seas might all be giving testimony of one form or another. What has the sky seen? What has the darkness of night recorded in its mind, regarding the sins of humanity? God's eyes are everywhere.

Lastly, Francis Schaeffer points out that by Joshua recording the words of the covenant, and writing down what he commanded of the people, we witness the expansion of the canon.[1] The word of God is spreading. There is now not only the words of Moses, but this new rock functioning as a transmitter that not only repeats the signal received from Moses, but includes the commentary and additions by Joshua. There is a progression of development regarding the canon of Scripture.

This passage provides good news about God. He does not change, and he hears and sees all things. The giving of his word was an act of ultimate condescension and grace. His word continues to stand, resolute and unchanging, marking the trajectory of the soul-migration of humans as they walk with him or away from him, especially those claiming to be his people. To understand the true treasure of Scripture is to see Christ in this rock of Joshua. He is the Rock that will hear the Rock and give the word of God back to God. Just as Jesus said that he only spoke what he heard from his Father (John 12:49) and he only did what the Father wanted (John 5:19, John 6:38), so the rock of Joshua will hear and bear witness to what the Father has said. There is no inscription upon this rock, because its single purpose is to show the Father.

O Word of God, Incarnate

(William Walsham How, 1867)

O Word of God incarnate,
O Wisdom from on high,
O Truth unchanged, unchanging,
O Light of our dark sky:
we praise you for the radiance
that from the Scripture's page,
a lantern to our footsteps,
shines on from age to age.

The church from you, dear Master,
received the gift divine;
and still that light is lifted
o'er all the earth to shine.

1. Schaeffer, *Joshua*, 204.

It is the chart and compass
that all life's voyage through,
mid mists and rocks and quicksands,
still guides, O Christ, to you.

O make your church, dear Savior,
a lamp of burnished gold
to bear before the nations
your true light as of old.
O teach your wandering pilgrims
by this our path to trace
till, clouds and darkness ended,
we see you face to face.

Chapter 12

Then Samuel took a stone and set it up between Mizpah and Shen and called its name Ebenezer; for he said, "Till now the Lord has helped us." (1 Sam 7:12)

SOMETIMES THE SCRIPTURES READ like a suspenseful scene from a horror film. By the time Israel has decided to turn from God and trust in their own strength, the reader begins to stress out. It's like the group of teenagers running from their attacker, when one of the girls decides to get out of the car and retrieve her phone from the house. "I know where it is. I'll be right back!" she assures her panic-stricken friends. Surely this isn't really happening?

Throughout the Old Testament, Israel is like this unnamed girl, sacrificed on the altar of cliches. Moments after having been saved from imminent death, she searches out the closest opportunity to squander her salvation. This portion of 1 Samuel 7 is a bit of fresh air. For a moment, Israel seems to have turned away from their own strength, and turned to God in genuine repentance and faith. It is a bright spot of faith in a sea of unbelief. There is an ancient and beautiful gesture that symbolizes their repentance. It is an acknowledgement of God's strength and worth, portrayed in the standing up of a stone in a field.

There is quite a bit of content that builds the context for 1 Samuel 7:12. In short, the people of Israel have put the Ark of the Covenant in storage at the house of a man named Abinidab. Abinidab's son, Eleazar, is placed in charge of it. The Scriptures tell us that it stayed in Kiriath-jearim for twenty years or so. During this time the people begin to experience a form of sorrow over their estrangement from the Living God. Samuel's voice rises to the fore and instructs the people that if they are genuine in their sorrow—meaning that their sorrow is directed towards God and not towards the negative effects of his absence—then they should turn their hearts to him.

Revival can be had if only God is that which is desired. The obedience that would flow from this genuine repentance, Samuel says, would take a certain shape. It should include the destruction of their idols, a heart-hunger after God, and a renewed worship of him alone. The people agree, and a nursing lamb is offered as a sacrifice. It is during this worship event that the Philistines hear about the people of Israel having gathered. Assuming that a crowd must be up to no good, they decide to attack. God sends a thundering that brings confusion into their midst and the enemy of Israel is defeated. The stone that is mentioned in this passage is erected and God's faithfulness to his people is proclaimed. The stone is called Ebenezer.

Unlike Joshua's raising of the stone by the tabernacle, back in Joshua, this raising of a stone is not to bear witness to the inevitable straying of the people from God; rather, this stone commemorates the reality of their homecoming. The name of the stone, "Ebenezer," is a word that is used preemptively by Samuel earlier in the book.

In 1 Samuel 4 and 5, the Ark of the Covenant was captured from the Israelites at Ebenezer, the place at which the Israelites had brought it into battle as a goodluck charm. This was the action that lost them the Ark. They trusted in the Ark to save them, rather than the God of the Ark. At the moment of the raising of Ebenezer, they have stopped trusting in anything other than God to help them. Ebenezer means "stone of help." They do not trust in the stone; rather, their repentance shows us they are trusting in the God who is symbolized by stone. The revival was not the direct object of their hunger, prayer, and yearning—God was the Direct Object. The revival was simply an adverb of their genuinely worshiping.

This is an important concept with ramifications for every generation of believers. When we pray for revival, are we panting after God or an experience having to do with God? Are we petitioning for himself or for a phenomenon? Would we who desire revival be content if God gave us himself outside the bounds of what we know to be revival?

Unlike the false repentance of Israel in Hosea 6, in which the people of God think that there can be a lateral returning to God without a vertical change, Israel in 1 Samuel 7 is genuinely turning to God. In Hosea 6, they are tired of the struggle. They want a break. Their wording is quite believable, but a careful reading reveals their true condition. They think of turning to God as the lesser of two evils: they can continue in their sin and reap the negative consequences, or they can swallow the bad medicine of repentance and hope the pain goes away.

> Come, let us return to the Lord; for he has torn us, that he may heal us; he has struck us down, and he will bind us up. After two days he will revive us; on the third day he will raise us up, that we may live before him. (Hos 6:1–2)

God is not convinced. Perceiving God as bad medicine, only slightly worth more than the sickness itself, is not to turn to God in repentance. It is as if God recites back to the them what they just said, but his inflection shows the deeper meaning. In chapter 7, he is accusing them of them of crying like babies, but not crying for their mama. They sure are promising a return to God, but only until the channel of their own contentment comes in clear again. They're moving, but not toward God. It looks like repentance, but it's just change.

> They do not cry to me from the heart, but they wail upon their beds; for grain and wine they gash themselves; they rebel against me. Although I trained and strengthened their arms, yet they devise evil against me. They return, but not upward. (Hos 7:14–16a)

Thankfully, that is not what is happening to Israel at Ebenezer. The very meaning of the name of the rock tells us the philosophy driving everything that's taking place. They are moving into a position of trusting in God and acknowledging their own helplessness. This is seen in an even fuller sense when a nursing lamb is sacrificed on a rock, just prior to the raising of Ebenezer. Both pieces of the worship event hold powerful signification. The nursing lamb, obviously, symbolizes a state of helpless dependency. As with all sacrifices, the offering is vicariously representative of the one giving it. For this reason, the impotence of the survivor is offered up to God on the rock. Throughout all of redemptive history, this would continue to be the structure of the great exchange, God gives us his steadfast and trustworthy strength and we give him our sin and helplessness.

Spurgeon ends up being no end of help regarding this passage. In a sermon he preached on March 15, 1863, he weaves many threads from this text together in order to show that the raising of Ebenezer is the commemoration of this one theme: God is sovereign and we should trust him *in* our helplessness, not simply in spite of it. He says there are three main qualities of the stone that should be considered: where it was raised, why it was raised, and the inscription upon it.[1]

It was raised on the very spot where so many had previously fallen. As stated, 1 Samuel 4 details the decision to bring the Ark of the Covenant amongst the people as a mascot of sorts. Clearly, treating the Living God as though he were a trinket will more than fail to bring about the desired consequences. Israel is slaughtered. Eli, the famous priest and father-figure to Samuel, has both of his sons killed. At nearly one hundred years old, and markedly overweight, he falls out of his chair when he hears the news and dies from a broken neck. His now-widowed daughter-in-law receives the news and is sent into labor. Her child is born premature and she designates him Ichabod, meaning "the glory has departed."

It was on the very field where so much devastation was administered that the stone is later raised. Again, the newfound creed is that they will trust in God from this day forward. This is declared in the very place they fell, because they previously did not trust in God. To trust in the gifts of God, the people of God, or the things of God is not the same thing as trusting in God. It should be remembered that the furniture of the Old Covenant existed to signify heavenly realities, not to mass-produce them.

> Now if he were on earth, he would not be a priest at all, since there are priests who offer gifts according to the law. They serve a copy and shadow of the heavenly things. For when Moses was about to erect the tent, he was instructed by God, saying, "See that you make everything according to the pattern that was shown you on the mountain." But as it is, Christ has obtained a ministry that is as much more excellent than the old as the covenant he mediates is better, since it is enacted on better promises. For if that first covenant had been faultless, there would have been no occasion to look for a second. (Heb 8:4–7)

In light of this, the sober reality is that placing one's trust in anything other than God—even godly things—is paganism of the highest order. This is taught throughout Scripture, but perhaps most notably in Romans 1. There are only two categories: created and Creator. The Israelites placed their trust in the created, rather than he who is signified by the created—that is, until the offering of the lamb. They were professing a faith in God and a repudiation of faith in anything else. They were needy, helpless, and worthy of death. The lamb, offered in their place, testified to this. The lamb and the

1. Spurgeon, "Ebenezer," lines 7–11.

rock: an image of the people of God, reconciled to God. The people are in the lamb.

The following verses show how efficacious this act of faith would be. They are immediately victorious. By the strength of God, they bring even those who had ruled over them into submission.

> And the men of Israel went out from Mizpah and pursued the Philistines and struck them, as far as below Beth-car. (1 Sam 7:11)

Spurgeon makes the observation that the name of the place Beth-car is translated "house of the lamb." It shows two important realities. Firstly, in a forthtelling way, it testifies to the fact that their victory truly came from all that was symbolized in the sacrificial lamb. Their acknowledgment to God that they were helpless and in need of his strength was affirmed by him. He brought their enemies into submission as far as the place of the lamb. In the King James Version, the phrase is "until they came under Beth-car." In light of this, we see the second reality. In more of a foretelling manner, we see that the greatest victory over any enemy would be to see them brought into submission under the Lamb as well. If it is a human adversary, we are to pray for this to be true. The death we are to desire is not of the whole person, but merely the adversary of faith which resides in the natural man. If the enemy is spiritual, like lust or greed, we are to desire its destruction by bringing it under the victory which is procured by the Lamb and is ours in him, because we are of his house. Sin is brought under us, because of the Lamb.

The raising of this stone, it must be remembered, did not incite any great response from God. The raising of Ebenezer was a response by the people to a great show of mercy by God. They had gathered for no other reason than worship. They came together to confess their sin and to return to God. The Philistines saw the gathering as an opportunity for greater oppression of Israel, but God had brought them to worship him, that he might give them deliverance.

To call the rock "stone of help" is to plainly acknowledge that it signifies God. They have learned their lesson about putting their faith in anything else. God, in his mercy, has brought his people to a place of humility. In this correct posture, his people of every time and place are brought to the same realization of John the Baptist: God must increase, and we must decrease. It is for this reason that the stone is raised, because it represents God, and everything else is being lowered by its raising.

The Philistines, who had esteemed themselves as greater than they ought to have, were lowered. The people of God who had esteemed themselves and other things as greater than they ought to have, were lowered. The stone, Ebenezer, symbolizing their God, was raised. This is precisely what is happening in every event of genuine worship.

Whether, as Spurgeon suggests, Samuel's statement upon the raising of Ebenezer was inscribed on the stone or merely uttered, is unclear. What *is* clear is that the utterance attributes all good things as having come from God: "Till now the Lord has helped us."

Spurgeon closes by making the contrast between a truly repentant Israel and Nebuchadnezzar, one of the great poster children of rebellion. Repentance raises God above the lowered heads of the crowd. Every rebel attempts to raise his or her head above the throne of God.

> And the king answered and said, "Is not this great Babylon, which
> I have built by my mighty power as a royal residence and for the
> glory of my majesty?" (Dan 4:30)

It is true in a number of languages that the words *humility* and *human* both find their origins in *humus*, or the earth. The words all share a common position, and that is non-Creator status. They are things that are made. Adam came from ground. To be humble is to be lowly or someone who is not raised up—above their position. All of this silently speaks to the status of the Creator. He is raised up. He is the only thing that ought to be raised up. We are weak. We are helpless. When God is worshiped in true faith and repentance, he gifts himself to his people. As they grow in their understanding of him, so should their voices grow. God is our help. He has helped us thus far.

Low at His Feet

(Daniel S. Warner, 1883)

Oh, when we remember the goodness
And infinite pity of God,
Who tenderly bore with our hardness,
When over His mercies we trod.

'Tis low, 'tis low,
Low down at His feet we bow;
'Tis low, 'tis low,
'Tis low at His feet we bow;

'Tis meet that a creature dependent
For even this breath that we draw,
Should feel very grateful, and humbly
Serve God in His beautiful law.

And when we behold the compassion
That flowed from the side of the Just;
Such love to the poor, guilty sinner
Compels us to fall in the dust.

Come, sinner, and ponder a moment,
The pains of the Crucified One;
Was not this to save thee from torment?
Then yield at the feet of the Son.

Chapter 13

"Oh that my words were written! Oh that they were inscribed in a book! Oh that with an iron pen and lead they were engraved in the rock forever! For I know that my Redeemer lives, and at the last he will stand upon the earth. And after my skin has been thus destroyed, yet in my flesh I shall see God, whom I shall see for myself, and my eyes shall behold, and not another. My heart faints within me!" (Job 19:23–27)

HALFWAY THROUGH THE BOOK of Job, we find this exasperated cry, sandwiched between the armchair life-coaching of Bildad and Zophar. Job is innocent, for the most part; however, his friends are working from the axiom that bad things don't happen to good people. They pelt him with accusations about hidden sin. When he responds with the confession of his guiltlessness, they accuse him of pride, thereby justifying their suspicions of him. With friends like this, who needs an online community?

It is in this crucible of friendly fire that Job cries out to the Lord. A number of theologians have worked tirelessly at dismantling the profundity of Job's exclamation in these verses, and weakening the obvious meaning of the text, for fear of putting too much eschatalogical weight on a solitary beam of Scripture. I'm speaking of the sparsity of Old Testament references to an afterlife. In this passage, it is not only Job's blatant mention of believing in a continuation of the self after death that is extremely rare, but also his mention of the inevitability of Job himself, while in the flesh, seeing God in the form of a Redeemer who will be standing upon the earth.

While the immediate inspiration for his utterance is the insult that is being added to the injury, it is necessary to remember that there is a more primary source of inspiration—the Holy Spirit. This passage is Scripture, breathed out by God, through the utterance of the man, Job. If the Scripture shows a consistency with the way in which rock and stone are employed throughout the Bible, what can a New Covenant Christian read in this passage, and recognize as gospel content? There are three components that will answer this question: the writing, the Redeemer, and the rock.

The Writing

> Oh that my words were written! Oh that they were inscribed in a book! Oh that with an iron pen and lead they were engraved in the rock forever!

In order to understand what Job is saying, we have to know the context. What are his words that he so wishes had some permanence and weight to them? There are two main options that we will consider: the primary statement made just *before* his request for his words to be recorded or the primary statement made just *after* his request for his words to be recorded. The former is as as follows:

> Have mercy on me, have mercy on me, O you my friends, for the hand of God has touched me! (Job 19:21)

The latter is the closing statement of the chapter, and renders it understandable why the chapter division was placed after this verse:

> Be afraid of the sword, for wrath brings the punishment of the sword, that you may know there is a judgment. (Job 19:29)

The first is a request for Job to receive mercy from his friends. The second is a warning for his friends to watch out, because judgment is real. Rather than seat these passages in opposition to one another, it would be far better to appeal first to the possibility of harmonization.

Job is exasperated and implores God in order that his words might be inscribed with metal upon stone. In reality, this request is a net that could be cast over nearly everything Job has said in the last nineteen chapters. Of course, in a way, this is a request that is granted by God, whether Job knew it or not. Job gives no indication that he understands his words would one day be canonized.

Even though our words do not hold the same weight as Scripture, every word each of us says is written with such eternal efficacy into an imprintable dimension of reality that we are guaranteed it will surface, later, at the judgment. The frivolous word we might deem "meaningless" does not slip through the screen; on the contrary, we are warned that it carries comparable weight to all the words we think matter.

> I tell you, on the day of judgment people will give an account for every careless word they speak, for by your words you will be justified, and by your words you will be condemned. (Matt 12:36–37)

When placed in the light of the gospel, it becomes obvious why Job might want his cry for mercy to be recorded in stone. It is a plea for justice. False accusations have been levied against him, and his heart wishes that an arbiter would weigh the factors fairly; however, the lesson of justification being a work of God is not learned fully by Job until the end of the book, but it is hinted at, even in his speech. Regardless of not being guilty of the charges, he is nonetheless guilty of believing his friends' prosperity gospel. He wants a justification earned by his own morality. In relation to his asking for everything he's ever said to be eternally recorded and called to the stand, we can only say, "Ye know not what ye ask." Listen to Adam Andrews on the subject:

> These passages provide a neat summary of the state of Job's heart: he remains convinced of his righteousness; he remains convinced that God is dealing unfairly with him; he all but accuses God of evading the question and withholding explanations. Job's faith is firmly anchored in his religion and his righteous conduct. He has pulled the levers well, and now demands from God an accounting.[1]

As I said, there is a hint that Job knows, or at least that the Spirit proclaims, that his hope should not lie in a fair trial, but in the trustworthiness of a Redeemer who has conquered death. We know this because he builds his conclusion that there should be a permanency to his innocence, due to the fact that his Redeemer lives and his flesh will be redeemed because of this. Just a few verses prior, he admits, regarding his own sinfulness, that, although he may be innocent of the charges brought against him, it is not intrinsic innocence that captures his ultimate hope—but the Living Redeemer. If all of this is due to sin, because God is good, he will not leave him here.

> And even if it be true that I have erred, my error remains with myself. If indeed you magnify yourselves against me and make my disgrace an argument against me, know then that God has put me in the wrong and closed his net about me. (Job 19:4–6)

1. Andrews, "The Seeing of the Eye," 23.

If Job is desiring that it be his warning of the coming judgment that is to be concretized, his message still holds up under translation into gospel vernacular. The gospel of an eternal justification for those who trust in the Redeemer is coupled with the warning that it is only death outside of him. He is our only hope in life and death. In keeping with the manner in which God uses rock and stone, self-referentially, it is safe to say that the Redeemer is the rock upon which the justification of the believer is written.

The Redeemer

In Isaiah 49, Isaiah is speaking prophetically about the Messiah, whom he calls the Redeemer of Israel. The work of this Servant is to bring hope and promise to those who are afflicted. Among the descriptions given are those who feel forsaken by God, those who have not been nursed by those who should have nursed them, those who sit in the dust, those who are bereaved, and those who live amidst the rubble of desolation. The promise concerning this Redeemer is that he will raise these sufferers out of their situation, if their hope is in his redemption.

It is into the cavern of this isolation that God declares they are not abandoned. Throughout the chapter, and especially at the end, the Redeemer is identified not only as a Servant of God, but as God himself.

> Then all flesh shall know that I am the Lord your Savior, and your Redeemer, the Mighty One of Jacob. (Isaiah 49:26b)

The parallels between Job 19 and Isaiah 49 are breathtaking. The existence of a Redeemer who, in some way, is greater than death, is the basis for Job's twofold outcry for his own justification and the warning of the coming judgment for others. This premise builds both the initial conclusion with which our passage started, and begins a new syllogism in which the Living Redeemer is also the foundation for Job's own flesh to both be destroyed and made new.

> For I know that my Redeemer lives, and at the last he will stand upon the earth. And after my skin has been thus destroyed, yet in my flesh I shall see God, whom I shall see for myself, and my eyes shall behold, and not another. My heart faints within me!

He is not only acquiescing to the fact that his skin being destroyed has some purpose and meaning in it; but he also argues that the flesh will be new and, on the earth, he will do what no one in the flesh is supposed to be able to do—see God. The Redeemer who could accomplish this, must, in harmony with Isaiah's assumption, not only be sent from God, but be God himself.

The Rock

Having seen both the permanent writing and the Redeemer being integrally related in the work of justification, set for us against the backdrop of judgment, as provided by his friends, we are brought to the final question: Who is this Rock?

Because of the eternal nature of the Redeemer, his words should be recorded. Despite any theological error on Job's part, this is ultimately a desire for his justification, to be sure. His conclusion is established on the premise that his Redeemer lives . . . specifically in a way that redeems those who belong to him from the permanency of death. The gospel tells us that his syllogism is sound. He, along with every believer after him, has a redemption that is sure because their Redeemer lives.

As we have seen in previous chapters, the Bible has already employed the imagery of eternal words written in stone. The Law of God is recorded on stone tablets. Since the Law of God was derived from the character of God, we can equate the rock, upon which the Law was written, to being the symbolic placeholder of God. Here, again, we are forced to assume that the only stone upon which Job's desire for justification could be written is the Lord God himself. Is there Biblical support for such a concept?

The presence of the rock is contrasted with the transitory nature of everything that doesn't last. That is why Job asks for his words to be recorded in stone and not in water. It is like he is filing a request with the Eternal to review his case. If this need for justification could someday make it to the judgment bench, God would vindicate the suffering. Going back to Isaiah 49, we see that there is not only a possibility of this happening, but a promise. His words will not only be recorded in stone, but on this Rock's very hands:

> Behold, I have engraved you on the palms of my hands. (Isa 49:16a)

Here Job contrasts the idea of personal tragedy with the immovable nature of stone. Everyone desires, in some way, to have something of weight, perhaps even glory, when faced with the removal of glory in suffering. At least that's what it seems like; but God turns suffering into glory. The promise of the Redeemer is that his elect will be written on his hands.

Job is perhaps the oldest book in the Bible, written long before the Law was given. There is no way he could be thinking about his own words becoming Scripture, and yet, here they are. They are set in stone, so to speak, alongside the commandments of God, written in stone. The eternal life of all that are written "in the Rock" is foreshadowed here, not only in his desire to see his words last, but in his subsequent statement about eternal life.

Those hands, upon which the names of the redeemed are written, were pierced with iron. It was the sin of the redeemed that called for the dictation. In this sense, we are the most vulgar of all graffiti artists. God, in his majesty, has retagged our work and redeemed it. What we meant for evil, God meant for good. Our malice has become a work of art, inscribed over by the love of God. It is as though the sinner could look at the cross, at the iron cuts in the Rock, and say at the very same time as Christ, "Look what I've done," and yet each mean two very different things. The truth is that, over time, his love drowns out the audible scream of our sin. It has to be that way. He sings harmony to our dissonance.

The Love of God

(Frederick M. Lehman, 1917)

The love of God is greater far
Than tongue or pen can ever tell;
It goes beyond the highest star,
And reaches to the lowest hell;

The guilty pair, bowed down with care,
God gave His Son to win;
His erring child He reconciled,
And pardoned from his sin.

Oh, love of God, how rich and pure!
How measureless and strong!
It shall forevermore endure—
The saints' and angels' song.

When hoary time shall pass away,
And earthly thrones and kingdoms fall,
When men who here refuse to pray,
On rocks and hills and mountains call,
God's love so sure, shall still endure,
All measureless and strong;
Redeeming grace to Adam's race—
The saints' and angels' song.

Could we with ink the ocean fill,
And were the skies of parchment made,
Were every stalk on earth a quill,
And every man a scribe by trade;
To write the love of God above
Would drain the ocean dry;
Nor could the scroll contain the whole,
Though stretched from sky to sky.

Chapter 14

O my dove, in the clefts of the rock,
in the crannies of the cliff,
let me see your face,
let me hear your voice,
for your voice is sweet,
and your face is lovely. (Song 2:14)

THE QUESTION THAT FACES us is one of how much New Testament pressure should be applied to Old Testament texts when interpreting them. To what degree should we think of all Scripture as centering on Christ? Clearly, one does not employ a one-to-one ratio and suggest that every verse is directly about Jesus. What he tells the disciples on the road to Emmaus is that if you start at the beginning of the Bible and work your way through, Jesus is regularly being discussed as the center of conversation—consistently and ubiquitously, we might say, but not exhaustively.

> And beginning with Moses and all the Prophets, He interpreted to them in all the Scriptures the things concerning Himself. (Luke 24:27)

Paul shows us how to do this well, as does the writer of Hebrews. The Song of Solomon is no exception. Christians will often err in one of two directions when it comes to The Song: either they make it only about Jesus and not sexual, or they make it only about sex and non-Christocentric. A harmony of the two is the correct path. This is one of the most remarkable and overlooked teachings of the Bible: sexual intimacy was created as a vehicle for the gospel.

In Ephesians 5, Paul begins the chapter by exhorting Christians to imitate God because of the gospel. He then sets in line with the truth of the gospel the reality that sexual purity should mark believers. Be sexually pure because of the gospel. This is his thinking:

> Therefore be imitators of God, as beloved children. And walk in love, as Christ loved us and gave himself up for us, a fragrant offering and sacrifice to God. But sexual immorality and all impurity or covetousness must not even be named among you, as is proper among saints. Let there be no filthiness nor foolish talk nor crude joking, which are out of place, but instead let there be thanksgiving. (Eph 5:1–4)

The gospel, Paul is saying, should inspire thankfulness and not impurity. One would not be out of line to understand thankfulness as being directed even toward sexuality. The truth is that sexual intimacy has long been a mystery. Because of this, and the fact that it holds such a central place in every human story, there is a temptation to exaggerate, abuse, and overextend its healthy boundaries. Don't do this, Paul says; rather, be thankful.

Covetousness is a part of this equation as well. Why do people's eyes wander? Because they allow themselves to want something they do not have, instead of being thankful for what they do have. This is not the only place in which the Bible speaks to thankfulness as being the godly antidote to sexual immorality:

> Drink water from your own cistern, flowing water from your own well. Should your springs be scattered abroad, streams of water in the streets? Let them be for yourself alone, and not for strangers with you. Let your fountain be blessed, and rejoice in the wife of your youth, a lovely deer, a graceful doe. Let her breasts fill you at all times with delight; be intoxicated always in her love. Why should you be intoxicated, my son, with a forbidden woman and embrace the bosom of an adulteress? For a man's ways are before the eyes of the Lord, and he ponders all his paths. (Prov 5:15–21)

Elsewhere, as well, God shows his anger towards those who allow covetousness to inspire ungratefulness in them, which will consistently manifest in sexual creatures as sexual immorality.

> And this second thing you do. You cover the Lord's altar with tears, with weeping and groaning because He no longer regards the offering or accepts it with favor from your hand. But you say, "Why does He not?" Because the Lord was witness between you and the wife of your youth, to whom you have been faithless, though she is your companion and your wife by covenant. Did He not make

them one, with a portion of the Spirit in their union? And what was the one God seeking? Godly offspring. So guard yourselves in your spirit, and let none of you be faithless to the wife of your youth. (Mal 2:13–15)

For this is the will of God, your sanctification: that you abstain from sexual immorality; that each one of you know how to control his own body in holiness and honor. (1 Thess 4:3–4)

Pleasure should produce gratitude. The danger of pleasure is that it can be pressured by sin into overextensions like gluttony, or perversions like masochism. Paul's reason for beginning Ephesians 5 by contrasting thankfulness with sexual impurity and covetousness is because he will end the chapter with the surprise statement that marriage, including sexual intimacy, has always been about Jesus and the church (his bride). It is for Christ's sake that he calls believers to thankfulness resulting in purity. Because Jesus is a certain kind of Husband, the church should be a certain kind of wife, a husband in the church should be a certain kind of husband, and a wife in the church should be a certain kind of wife. The line extends from the gospel, straight through the communion table, and into the marriage bed:

Therefore a man shall leave his father and mother and hold fast to his wife, and the two shall become one flesh." This mystery is profound, and I am saying that it refers to Christ and the church. (Eph 5:31–32)

What refers to Christ and the church? The sexual union that is at the center of marriage is analogously our own hypostasis in which multiplicity is housed by singularity. With the Biblical structure in place, we see that sexual intimacy is not only the design of God for accomplishing procreation, but it is also pleasurable by design because it signifies the joy of the believer's union with Christ. From Proverbs to Malachi to 1 Thessalonians and Ephesians, the Bible establishes marriage-bed intimacy as being directly related to the gospel. With this in mind, our passage from Song of Solomon begins to yield her fruit:

O my dove, in the clefts of the rock, in the crannies of the cliff, let me see your face, let me hear your voice, for your voice is sweet, and your face is lovely.

The speaker is the bride, but the words are the words of her husband. She is preaching to herself what he has told her to be true. She is reminding herself of the ways in which he values and desires her. Right desire is the basis for the right kind of jealousy. Of course, there are perversions of both desire and jealousy, but a wife who values being rightly desired by her husband should know an assurance and joy that is shared between them both.

This chapter houses two instances of imagery in which the husband is feasting upon his bride in the context of cleavage. In verse 14, the cleavage is representative of the place which is hiding the lover from the hungry eyes of her husband who desires to see her form. In verse 17, she sheds her coyness and encourages him to feast on her like a stag in the cleavage of the mountains.

> My beloved is mine, and I am his; he grazes among the lilies. Until the day breathes and the shadows flee, turn, my beloved, be like a gazelle or a young stag on cleft mountains. (Song 2:16–17)

Lest anyone think this crass, it should be restated that sexual intimacy is not dirty nor immoral, if discussed in a godly fashion. That is, after all, proven by the fact that the Song of Solomon is God-breathed Scripture. The very refrain of the song is that one not awaken this thing until its proper place and time; but it is beautiful and ecstatic when awakened appropriately.

The bride knows that her husband desires her to open up to him. As I said previously, she is preaching the truth of his words to herself, and the result of her doing so is her invitation and expressed desire for intimacy, as seen in verse 17. The Christian would do well to model this in his or her own life. The truth that God desires his bride must never be downplayed— not because there is some inherent value in us—but because he has imputed genuine value to us by his choice. To deny this is to be unbelieving.

In New Covenant language, the Christian overcomes her lack of intimacy with God by preaching the gospel to herself. God so loved his people that he pursues them, even to the point of bleeding and dying for them. She tells herself, like the depressed psalmist, that God wants her to come out of hiding, and by believing his word, she emerges from her den. Do you lack intimacy? Do you preach the truth of God's love to yourself until you open to him?

> The LORD your God is in your midst, a mighty one who will save; He will rejoice over you with gladness; He will quiet you by his love; He will exult over you with loud singing. (Zeph 3:17)

The line from marriage to the gospel is drawn by the fact that God desires his people and he thinks monogamously about only his people. His bride, the church, is the sole object of his love and pursuit.

Now, as I said, there are two differing images of cleavage in Song of Solomon 2. In verse 14, it is cleavage that hides the reticent lover from her husband. The image that comes to mind is that of a nervous infant burrowing his face into his mother's breasts in order to shy away from a stranger.

A mentor of mine told me of an ancient story he read when visiting the Bodleian Library. There was a people who lived on the high cliffs of a certain land. The women of this group were shepherdesses. They raised their children from birth amidst their work of tending the sheep. When any of the children would wander too close to the edge of the dangerous cliffs, the mother would not run towards the child; rather, she would undo her shirt and expose her breast to the little one, who would toddle away from danger, toward the source of safety and comfort.

The breasts are a place of safety and rest. The dove is hiding there. Moses was placed there. This cleavage creates a distance between two things. In Song of Solomon it creates distance between the lovers, and in Exodus it places distance between the deadly glory of God and fragility of Moses' frame. Of course, in both instances, the cleft is between two layers of rock, but the cleavage in both instances is used to create a greater cleavage.

> And the Lord said, "Behold, there is a place by me where you shall stand on the rock, and while my glory passes by I will put you in a cleft of the rock, and I will cover you with my hand until I have passed by. Then I will take away my hand, and you shall see my back, but my face shall not be seen." (Exodus 33:21–23)

In verse 17 of our Song of Solomon passage, the cleavage is between two mountains, but it is employed as an invitation for intimacy. This is possible because of the complexity of the word *cleave*, which means both to sever and to bond. A husband and wife are to cleave to one another, but marriage is a cleaver that adjures them to forsake all others. It is not accidental that the Bible uses this word in all its fullness to describe the sexual identity of the man. He is to experience two forms of cleavage: the first is from his mother, and the second is to his wife. Both the safety and refuge of the nursing infant and the ecstasy of the lover are to be found by the husband in the breasts of his wife, and no longer in the figurative breasts of his mother.

> Therefore shall a man leave his father and his mother, and shall
> cleave unto his wife: and they shall be one flesh. (Gen 2:24, KJV)

Marriage is a cleaver that descends between the man and his mother, and has placed a deep ravine betwixt them. In marriage, however, the man finds that he is not alone on his side of the ravine; rather, his wife is stranded on that side with him. This is good in God's sight. Now, all things feminine are to be found in the sole fountain that is his wife. Remember the the admonition of Solomon to young men in Proverbs 5:

> Let your fountain be blessed, and rejoice in the wife of your youth,
> a lovely deer, a graceful doe. Let her breasts fill you at all times with
> delight; be intoxicated always in her love. (Prov 5:18–19)

The doe of Proverbs meets the stag of Song of Solomon in the pleasure of the marriage bed. This is syntopical harmony that one should expect if the gospel is the unifying theme of all Scripture, which leads us to the most important application of the text: that truer and greater refuge and joy are to be found more in God than they are in the greatest of wives.

Both male and female were created in the image of God. This is not to say that God identifies himself in the feminine. He does not; neither should he ever be identified by anyone in the feminine. He is the primary archetype of sexuality from which both the image of male and female are derived. But even having said this, it is crucial that the order be maintained. The feminine was created with something that was taken from the masculine. This was then positioned in such a manner as to complement the masculine. The feminine is a response to the masculine. This is why God could never be identified in the feminine, because it would be like saying, "Hear, oh Israel, the Lord, the Lord your God is two."

However, once this is established, we are freed up to understand the origins of the feminine. Female humanity was made in the image of God. Because this is true of both female and male humanity, this combined with the fact that God, who is Spirit, identifies in the masculine, tells us that sexual identity is something that goes much deeper than physicality. God is Spirit. Because sexual identity is a part of his image, it must be deeper than the reach of the scalpel.

The horizontal truth should teach us a greater vertical truth. The horizontal, properly understood, signifies the vertical. It is true that all creation, properly understood, signifies attributes of the Creator. It is no less true that horizontal vehicles of covenantal sensuality, properly understood, signify a greater vertical source of peace and ecstasy. In this sense, the breasts of God are more satisfying than those of one's wife. Again, this is not meant in a way that feminizes God, but in a way that, when properly understood, shows the divine origins of femininity. What could the breasts of a perfect wife ever give a man? Peace? Refuge? Joy? Sustenance? God gives this, but more so. In fact, as Paul tells us, the mystery is that the sexual union is actually a signifier of the believer's union with Christ. This is the only eternal marriage. This is the marriage to which every earthly marriage, including the most godly and heroic, are mere echoes.

Remember how Song of Solomon 2 begins, by the bride declaring herself to be the rose of sharon and the lily of the valley. If the reader were to solely equate the church with the feminine counterpart to the pursuing groom, then it would be fair for the church to also think of herself as the rose of sharon and the lily of the valley. Thankfully, the church has rightly understood the correlation, but not stopped there. Why? Because whatever is truth on the horizontal plain is more so on the vertical. The church has historically understood that it is more correct to think of this object of beauty and desire as being Jesus, far more than it is the church, even though it is the church in a lesser way. That is why the hymn says, "He's the Lily of the Valley," taken from the opening of this chapter about the Bride, and not "We're the Lily of the Valley." Could you imagine singing the praises of yourself? God forbid. The gospel makes it plain. Jesus is the Rose of Sharon, the sweet flower of the barren land, the Lily of the Valley. He is the bright and morning star. We are told that his countenance on the New Earth renders the sun unnecessary, because he is more light than the sun. He is more Israel than Israel. He's the central theme of the works of God and the word of God. He is the merging point of God and humanity. He is the focal point of all true worship. His is the strength and honor of the bridegroom and the desirability and beauty of the bride.

Lily of the Valley

(Charles W. Frye, 1881)

I've found a friend in Jesus, He's everything to me,
He's the fairest of ten thousand to my soul;
The Lily of the Valley, in Him alone I see
All I need to cleanse and make me fully whole.

In sorrow He's my comfort, in trouble He's my stay;
He tells me every care on Him to roll.

He's the Lily of the Valley, the Bright and Morning Star,
He's the fairest of ten thousand to my soul.

He all my grief has taken, and all my sorrows borne;
In temptation He's my strong and mighty tower;
I've all for Him forsaken, and all my idols torn
From my heart and now He keeps me by His pow'r.
Though all the world forsake me, and Satan tempt me sore,
Through Jesus I shall safely reach the goal.

He'll never, never leave me, nor yet forsake me here,
While I live by faith and do His blessed will;
A wall of fire about me, I've nothing now to fear,
From His manna He my hungry soul shall fill.
Then sweeping up to glory to see His blessed face,
Where rivers of delight shall ever roll.

Chapter 15

You saw, O king, and behold, a great image. This image, mighty and of exceeding brightness, stood before you, and its appearance was frightening. The head of this image was of fine gold, its chest and arms of silver, its middle and thighs of bronze, its legs of iron, its feet partly of iron and partly of clay. As you looked, a stone was cut out by no human hand, and it struck the image on its feet of iron and clay, and broke them in pieces. Then the iron, the clay, the bronze, the silver, and the gold, all together were broken in pieces, and became like the chaff of the summer threshing floors; and the wind carried them away, so that not a trace of them could be found. But the stone that struck the image became a great mountain and filled the whole earth. (Dan 2:31–35)

In one of the brightest spots of redemptive history, the Babylonian emperor, Nebuchadnezzar, had a dream that was very troubling to him. As if burnt out on the parlor tricks and horoscopic ambiguity of his wise men and suffering under the weight of this dream, he demanded that someone from among his counselors tell him, not only the interpretation of the dream, but also the dream itself. There was no one who could meet this demand. Hearing of Nebuchadnezzar's imminent plan to have every sage in Babylon torn limb from limb, Daniel approached his countrymen, Hananiah, Mishael, and Azariah, asking them to pray to God for their salvation. During the night, Daniel was given a dream of the dream and its interpretation. Verses 31–35 of chapter 2 describe Daniel presenting the dream to the ruler. He then proceeds to give the correct interpretation:

This was the dream. Now we will tell the king its interpretation. You, O king, the king of kings, to whom the God of heaven has given the kingdom, the power, and the might, and the glory, and into whose hand he has given, wherever they dwell, the children of man, the beasts of the field, and the birds of the heavens, making you rule over them all—you are the head of gold. Another kingdom inferior to you shall arise after you, and yet a third kingdom of bronze, which shall rule over all the earth. And there shall be a fourth kingdom, strong as iron, because iron breaks to pieces and shatters all things. And like iron that crushes, it shall break and crush all these. And as you saw the feet and toes, partly of potter's clay and partly of iron, it shall be a divided kingdom, but some of the firmness of iron shall be in it, just as you saw iron mixed with the soft clay. And as the toes of the feet were partly iron and partly clay, so the kingdom shall be partly strong and partly brittle. As you saw the iron mixed with soft clay, so they will mix with one another in marriage, but they will not hold together, just as iron does not mix with clay. And in the days of those kings the God of heaven will set up a kingdom that shall never be destroyed, nor shall the kingdom be left to another people. It shall break in pieces all these kingdoms and bring them to an end, and it shall stand forever, just as you saw that a stone was cut from a mountain by no human hand, and that it broke in pieces the iron, the bronze, the clay, the silver, and the gold. A great God has made known to the king what shall be after this. The dream is certain, and its interpretation sure. (Dan 2:36–45)

Daniel was one of the Hebrew children who was taken into Babylonian captivity by Nebuchadnezzar in 586 BC. Like Joseph before him, he rose to the higher ranks of political power in the land of his captivity. Daniel saw the overthrow of the Babylonian empire by the Medo-Persians, and was famously delivered safe and sound from the lion's den by the mercy of God; thusly, inspiring a profession of belief in the God of Israel by Darius the Mede and the subsequent execution of those involved in the plot against Daniel.

The image is representative of world empires. We are told that the gold head is Nebuchadnezzar's empire. History tells us the Medo-Persian empire is the one that is silver, following Babylon's gold. The Greek empire, under Alexander the Great, displaced the Persians. Rome followed Greece, and it is after the displacement of Rome by a fissuring that a multitude of nations, some strong and some weak, some unified and some divided, will welcome the global arrival of the kingdom of God and their own disappearance act.

There is a particular phrase that Daniel uses in relation to Nebuchadnezzar. For a season, God has given this ruler, whom he calls the "King of Kings," the kingdom, the power, and the glory. He says that God has not only given him this glory, but he has also given him dominion over creation, for a season. Any reader of Scripture knows that these are things which rightly belong to God. Daniel undoubtedly learns about this status being attributed to Nebuchadnezzar by God, not only from the dream, but also from what we know was his contemplative reading of the prophecy of Jeremiah.

> Give them this charge for their masters: "Thus says the Lord of hosts, the God of Israel: This is what you shall say to your masters: 'It is I who by my great power and my outstretched arm have made the earth, with the men and animals that are on the earth, and I give it to whomever it seems right to me. Now I have given all these lands into the hand of Nebuchadnezzar, the king of Babylon, my servant, and I have given him also the beasts of the field to serve him. All the nations shall serve him and his son and his grandson, until the time of his own land comes. Then many nations and great kings shall make him their slave.'" (Jer 27:4–7)

This arrangement isn't forever. It is like the seasonal lease of a field, with the terms being defined by God. God says to Jeremiah that this glory and dominion will be given to the ruler of Babylon until the time of his own land comes to pass—or until the trophy and glory are passed on to the new reigning champs.

When I was in high school, my martial arts instructor had gone away for a week, leaving the keys to the studio with my friends and I who spent most of our time there. His many-degreed instructor's belt was left hanging over the railing in the front of the room. Being the class clown that I was in those days, I put the belt on and pretended to be a world-class martial artist. When he returned from vacation one of my friends decided to tell him what I'd done in his absence. He showed up one afternoon at my house and asked to speak to my father and me. He told my dad that he was requesting permission to challenge me to defend my belt. Of course, he didn't mean the belt level I actually held; he was alluding to the hypocrisy of my wearing his belt—a belt level to which I was not entitled.

You can imagine Nebuchadnezzar being in a similar spot. There is this wild season in which he is being called the king of kings, and being told by wisemen that the kingdom and the power and the glory are all his. In the history of empire, the Biblical record tells us that no one will succeed at outshining the glory of Nebuchadnezzar's Babylon. This is hard for many of us to fathom, living in an era of great wealth and technological advancement.

It raises an important conversation about the nature of empire and its relationship with eschatology; however, for our purposes, it should not be forgotten that Rome is cataloged as iron compared with Babylon's gold. Jeremiah is told by God that because Nebuchadnezzar is not really a god, there will be a day in which he is forced to defend his belt. Of course, this is a battle he will lose.

There is a lease on these properties of kingdom, power, and glory which God gives to rulers throughout the ages of the Earth. There is a shared spirit behind those who hold these things. It unifies rulers of empire throughout history. It imprints upon them similar methodologies and inspirations. The devil is described as being the supracultural lessee who transcends ages of empires and geographic boundaries. He sublets these properties, per the will of God, to temporal shareholders:

> And the devil took him up and showed him all the kingdoms of
> the world in a moment of time, and said to him, "To you I will give
> all this authority and their glory, for it has been delivered to me,
> and I give it to whom I will. If you, then, will worship me, it will all
> be yours." (Luke 4:5–7)

Jesus knew the temporary nature of the devil's claim to dominion. The testimony of Scripture is that all the kingdoms will indeed be Christ's, but they will be handed over to him by God and not the devil. The true owner of the worldwide vineyard is God, not the tenant farmer who has forgotten this during his years of renting.

In the Daniel passage, we are told that, when this little stone of a kingdom—which is clearly the kingdom of God—starts to take over the Earth in its active and advancing form, it is at the level of the mixed-nation empire, after the end of the Roman one. Jesus dies approximately four hundred years before Rome falls. In those first hundred years of the church, there was a worldwide announcing of God as King that has only grown since then. The gap between the announcement of the arrival of the kingdom and those who have not heard it is shrinking every day.

We have seen how the greatest moments of Western civilization have been birthed by the imprint of Christianity upon progress. The wake that moved out of Jerusalem, just after the ascension of Christ, was most widely received westwardly. Now, in our day, the world is poised in anticipation as the proclamation of the kingdom of God is most profoundly received in the East and in the South. It cannot be doubted that it is filling the Earth.

The rock that was not hewn by any human hand is none other than the kingdom of God. Daniel says this in the interpretation that is given of the dream.

> And in the days of those kings the God of heaven will set up a kingdom that shall never be destroyed, nor shall the kingdom be left to another people. It shall break in pieces all these kingdoms and bring them to an end, and it shall stand forever, just as you saw that a stone was cut from a mountain by no human hand, and that it broke in pieces the iron, the bronze, the clay, the silver, and the gold.

God will set up a kingdom. The Scriptures ubiquitously teach us that the Rock upon which this kingdom is built is none other than Christ himself; hence, his having not been cut by human hands. In this case, the Stone is, again, an Icon of the Mountain.

In Matthew 21, the chapter begins by announcing Jesus as the fulfillment of the Zechariah 9 prophecy, in which Judah is told to look at the long-awaited King approaching on a donkey. Jesus is praised as the royal promise of David's line in his triumphal entry into Jerusalem. He then withdraws to Bethany and tells two parables about a man who owns a vineyard. In the second parable, the main plot is the displacement of rulers who had no right to reign as lords.

> Jesus said to them, "Have you never read in the Scriptures: 'The stone that the builders rejected has become the cornerstone; this was the Lord's doing, and it is marvelous in our eyes'? Therefore I tell you, the kingdom of God will be taken away from you and given to a people producing its fruits. And the one who falls on this stone will be broken to pieces; and when it falls on anyone, it will crush him." (Matt 21:42–44)

This is the announcement of the kingdom of God. Jesus is the King, and it is impossible to miss that his message, and the message of his disciples, was that the long-awaited kingdom had arrived. That kingdom of God is anywhere God reigns as King; but the arrival that many, including Joseph of Arimathea, had been waiting for was what the kingdom would do in its arrival—it would displace all other kingdoms.

It is common to assume that Jesus must have surely disappointed everyone in Israel by not driving out Rome in his arrival. In truth, some even refused to believe that he was the Messiah for lack of proof that he was displacing the earthly rulers. There is a ditch on both sides of the road here. One ditch responds to this by saying, "Well, he isn't going to displace earthly rulers in his first advent, but he will in his second." The other ditch is that some will run to employ the Law of Moses as the means by which pagan rulers will be displaced.

The gospel will be the lever that pries pagan emperors from their thrones. Rome was displaced as a great empire almost immediately after Theodosius's declaration of Christianity as the official religion of Rome. Many who see this as tragic blame Christianity for destroying the empire-wide binding agent of pagan culture which held Rome together. The displacement is not over, clearly. The truth is that Christ did not fail to displace Rome as foreign occupier; rather, it's merely that his first advent had a soft opening. He is in the middle of that work of displacing empires even now. The stone, remember, struck the feet of Nebuchadnezzar's image, not the legs. The feet were the divided nations that are reminiscent of Rome, vying for the greatness of Rome, but consistently failing to achieve it. No empire in existence today will succeed to reclaim the glory of Rome; not a New World Order, United Nations, nor the United States. The kingdom of God has arrived on Earth, and the empires will only continue to crumble, until they are dust and are never heard from again.

For two thousand years the kingdom of God has been both "already and not yet." This means that the "not yet" quadrant has been shrinking steadily. The good news is that this is not anybody's game. This kingdom, of which every Christian on the planet proclaims the gospel, is not going to recede. It is advancing. It will fill the Earth and never be displaced, we are told. It may be not yet, but is a good deal already.

Jesus Shall Reign Where'er the Sun

(Isaac Watts, 1719)

Jesus shall reign where're the sun does his successive journeys run;
His kingdom spread from shore to shore, til moons shall wax and wane no more.

From north to south the princes meet to pay their homage at His feet;
While western empires own their Lord, and savage tribes attend His Word.

To Him shall endless prayer be made, and endless praises crown His head;
His Name like sweet perfume shall rise with every morning sacrifice.

People and realms of every tongue dwell on His love with sweetest song,
And infant voices shall proclaim their early blessings on His Name.

Chapter 16

And I tell you, you are Peter, and on this rock I will build my church, and the gates of hell shall not prevail against it. (Matt 16:18)

JESUS IS OFTEN ACCUSED by his critics as being someone who never laughed; at least, there is no Biblical record of him having laughed. Usually, this is called to the stand as testimony of his being a man without a sense of humor. This is a big deal, of course, because a man without a sense of humor can't be trusted. There's something non-human about it. Thankfully, it's impossible to read the Scriptures and come away from them with a view of Jesus being anything but a lover of humor and wit.

No doubt, he is a man of many sorrows (Isa 53:3). No doubt, he understands more than any other that it is better to go into a house of mourning than a house of feasting (Eccl 7:2). But we must not forget that Jesus also loved feasting—so much so, that he was accused of being a drunkard and a glutton (Matt 11:19). A careful reading of Scripture will reveal to us that, in the margins, there is also the Christ of hyperbole and witty comebacks.

Whether it's his description of the hypocrite with a plank sticking out of his eye or the image of a rich man trying to squeeze a camel through an eye of a needle, Jesus regularly strikes us as someone with a flair for repartee. Dare we even say sarcasm? How many times did he say something that elicited a chuckle? We don't know, because the chuckles aren't recorded; but, thankfully, the sharp one-liners are.

This exchange with Peter is no exception. The content couldn't be of higher importance. Jesus is discussing the construction of his church and his plan for the future, including the inevitable exiling of death and decay from the New Earth. This is truly a doctrine with weighty consequences;

however, Jesus doesn't shy away from making wordplay a part of how he will talk about the success of the kingdom.

The reason the proper interpretation for this passage has long been argued over is precisely because of this wordplay. It is genuinely a case of someone speaking in layers and everyone who reads the transcript arguing amongst themselves as to which layer is the interpretive one for the others. Thankfully, if we take one possible meaning at a time, each examined on its own, it becomes clear that only one interpretation of the rock can be the ultimate answer, even if the others hold an element of merit.

Jesus and his disciples have entered Caesarea Philippi and, while they are there, he asks his disciples what other people are saying about him. Like the passage in hand, there are differing opinions being asserted. He then asks them directly what they themselves say about him. Peter is bold enough to announce Jesus as the Messiah, come from God:

> Now when Jesus came into the district of Caesarea Philippi, he asked his disciples, "Who do people say that the Son of Man is?" And they said, "Some say John the Baptist, others say Elijah, and others Jeremiah or one of the prophets." He said to them, "But who do you say that I am?" Simon Peter replied, "You are the Christ, the Son of the living God." And Jesus answered him, "Blessed are you, Simon Bar-Jonah! For flesh and blood has not revealed this to you, but my Father who is in heaven." (Matt 16:13–17)

The verse that follows, containing the rock's shared territory with Peter's name, is a response by Jesus to the fact that Peter has correctly identified him as the long-prophesied Messiah and the Son of the Living God. This should be kept in mind. Jesus acknowledges that, left to his own devices, Peter would not have gotten this right—but, praise God, he did get it right. The reader of verse 18 must keep the same lightbulb on that burned so brightly in verses 13–17. Proper identification is a big deal. Any praise Peter is given is based on Peter's correct view of Christ as the Son of God.

Each candidate for the rock in question has a historical case, rooted in viability; but only Christ as the Rock holds the highest interpretive collateral. Christ is, undeniably, the ultimate Rock upon which the church is built. Any rock that could potentially be a contender could only exist as a signifier of the truer Rock. Whether it be Peter himself, his confession, or the bare ground near the pagan cave at Caesarea Philippi, all are mere types or signifiers of Christ, because the primary target is the Rock upon which the church is built. This means that, whether Jesus poked his finger in Peter's chest or stomped his foot on the entrance to the Cave of the Gods, when he said "this rock," his use of wordplay carries us along, inevitably, until we arrive at the feet of a Rock above which no higher rock could ever be conceived. That Rock, as Peter will later say, is Jesus.

There is an extensive conversation that has stretched thousands of years amongst linguists and scholars concerning nuances of the Greek and Aramaic words for stone and rock and the finer points of the dative case. From what I gather, if Jesus meant to call Peter the rock on which he would build his church, he sure said it weirdly. In English, we feel the speed-bump in the use of the determiner *this*. Jesus could have said something like, "You are Peter, and on *you*, the Rock, I will build my church." He could have said, "This is Peter, the Rock, and on *him* I'm going to build my church." The fact that he didn't say it in a plainer manner tells us that the ambiguity isn't accidental. We're not dealing with someone who doesn't know how to speak. He is the Living Word, after all.

With this in mind, we recognize that Peter is most assuredly *a* rock, although it is impossible for him to be *the* rock on which the church is built. Firstly, if we look at the picture of the heavenly city, in Revelation, we see that the apostles' names are written on the foundation stones. Those stones are the stones on which the entire city is built.

> And the wall of the city had twelve foundations, and on them were the twelve names of the twelve apostles of the Lamb. (Rev 21:14)

We know from other passages, like 1 Peter 2:5, that believers are living stones that are built together into the spiritual house for the Living God. This is the picture being developed in Revelation 21. Clearly, based on his 1 Peter imagery, this picture has been in Peter's head for years—long after Jesus reminds him of the name Jesus himself assigned him: Peter, which means "rock."

> You yourselves like living stones are being built up as a spiritual house, to be a holy priesthood, to offer spiritual sacrifices acceptable to God through Jesus Christ. (1 Pet 2:5)

When we read either of Peter's letters, we see a man who identifies himself as being a part of the corpus of followers, and in no way distinguishes himself from that lot of living stones. The issue of Peter holding some sort of special office is a non-existent issue in the history of the church, until the second century. Peter was an overseer and an apostle, and those are special roles, but they are not unique to Peter.

Peter goes on to say who the only special stone is—and it is not any one of the apostles. This stands in opposition to every reader who would argue that the rock being referred to in Jesus' statement is Peter. The apostles are foundation stones, to be sure; but they are foundation stones that rest against the Cornerstone—upon which the church is built. Imagine if Peter had mentioned himself as the stone upon which the church would be built. The blasphemy.

> For it stands in Scripture: "Behold, I am laying in Zion a stone, a cornerstone chosen and precious, and whoever believes in him will not be put to shame." So the honor is for you who believe, but for those who do not believe, "The stone that the builders rejected has become the cornerstone," and "A stone of stumbling, and a rock of offense." (1 Pet 2:6–8a)

So, there is no issue with suggesting that Peter is a stone of sorts. There is plenty of Scriptural support of this. The issue, however, remains that Peter is a stone in the same way other believers are stones. The only distinction that could be attributed to Peter is that he is one of the first foundational layers. Other stones (the church) absolutely are laid on top of him, but if one uses Revelation 21:14 as a lens through which to see Peter as the stone upon which the church is built, then it is built on the other eleven apostles equally sharing the load. In that sense, Jesus must have said, or at least meant, something similar to every other apostle as well; e.g., "You are Nathaniel, and on you 'God has given' to have his church built." He is *a* rock upon which the church is built, but that doesn't make sense of the singularity of the rock and the singularity of the determiner in Christ's statement.

It is all clumsy because the grammar doesn't seem to work seamlessly. But it is clumsy only if we are trying to make a unique role for Peter, which exegesis and history cannot be wrangled into making for him. It is possible to see that there is a correlation between Peter being identified by Jesus as a kind of rock, Peter properly confessing Jesus as the Son of God, and Jesus responding by saying that Peter would play an important role in the building of his church, because Rock calls out to rock.

The same kind of clumsiness emerges if we try to have Peter's confession alone become the rock that Jesus identifies with the determiner *this*. He could have easily said, "You are Peter, the Rock, and on the profession you've just made I will build my church." That would be a little more readable, grammatically speaking, but two things would be insinuated. The first would be that, because that is not how he said it, Jesus just ain't talk good. The second thing would be that Peter's profession of Jesus as the Messiah is the foundation of the church. That's not the worst candidate for the job, by far. In fact, a pretty solid case can and has been made for this reading. The profession of Christ as Lord is most certainly the birthmark of orthodoxy:

> Because, if you confess with your mouth that Jesus is Lord and believe in your heart that God raised him from the dead, you will be saved. (Rom 10:9)

The concern isn't whether or not professing Jesus as Lord is a foundational issue. Clearly it is foundational. The question is whether or not the Lord is genuinely calling Peter's profession the rock upon which the church is built. It's not simply the awkward syntax that leaves this theory on the scales found wanting, even though the argument can be made for aspects of Greek syntax being lost in translation; indeed, scholars and linguists have made such arguments.

No different than the Ark of the Covenant being lost to the Philistines in 1 Samuel because of the superstitious manner in which Israel treated the Ark, to suggest that the profession of Peter is the rock upon which the church is built, when clearly there is a Rock upon which the church is built that is far more foundational, seems to be a bit of the old swearing by the throne rather than him who sits upon it. The profession of Christ as Lord isn't the rock upon which the church is built, not in the same way that Christ is the Rock upon which the church is built.

But there is still a third-party candidate: Panias, now called Banias, also known as Caesarea Philippi, was home to a cave that guarded a pool from which the Jordan River flowed and Gennesaret and the Sea of Galilee were both filled. It was called Panias when it was the location of a temple dedicated to Pan, Echo, and Hermes. Residences for Caesar Augustus and Herod Agrippa were built there as well. This was the claim to fame of Caesarea Philippi—the very place in which Jesus and his disciples are having this discourse. The locals called this cave the "Gates of Hades"[1]—the exact phrase that is put in the English as the "Gates of Hell."

---

1. Josephus, "Of the War—Book III," http://penelope.uchicago.edu/josephus/war-3. html.

The relevance of the location on which Jesus is standing when speaking the words "this rock" is compounded when we realize that he is in Panias (Caesarea Philippi) and he has referenced the gates of Hades. To fail to recognize these details would seem to be an irresponsible approach to understanding the text. The grammar and syntax end up flowing nicely.

The determiner makes sense, as does the connection between Peter's name and the rock on which they are both standing. It must also be said that the region of Galilee, especially the northern part, to which Caesarea Philippi belonged, is a profoundly important region. It is the region designated by prophecy to be where the Messiah would introduce his kingdom of light. It is from this northern region, widely rejected by faithful Israel because of the influence of the pagan border countries, that Christ would call almost all of his disciples. In a very real sense, the work of the church began on that northern rock—the very spot where Israel touches the rest of the world. In making sense of Panias and other towns in Israel's northern territory, Alfred Edersheim explains that this is the reason for its being called "Galilee of the Gentiles."

> For the present it will suffice to remark, that north-eastern or Upper Galilee was in great part inhabited by Gentiles-Phoenicians, Syrians, Arabs, and Greeks (Josephus, *Jewish War*, iii, 419-427), whence the name "Galilee of the Gentiles" (Matt 4:15). It is strange in how many even of those cities, with which we are familiar from the New Testament, the heathen element prevailed.[2]

Prophecy is being fulfilled in Jesus' initiating the announcement of the gospel of the kingdom in this territory, on this rock. The calling of his first disciples was in Galilee of the Gentiles. His first significant wonder was performed at the wedding in Cana, in Galilee of the Gentiles. Listen to the words of Scripture, concerning the region upon which Jesus and the disciples are standing when he announces that on "this rock" he would build his church:

> But there will be no gloom for her who was in anguish. In the former time he brought into contempt the land of Zebulun and the land of Naphtali, but in the latter time he has made glorious the way of the sea, the land beyond the Jordan, Galilee of the nations. The people who walked in darkness have seen a great light; those who dwelt in a land of deep darkness, on them has light shone. (Isa 9:1–2)

2. Edersheim, *Sketches of Jewish Social Life*, 15.

It should be easily agreed upon that the introduction of light into this dark region is fulfilled in the ministry of Christ to the people held in dark bondage there. In fact, as already stated, he would build his church with workers from this shadowland. Now, if we introduce the fulfillment of the Isaiah 9 passage as being the work and person of Jesus, from his preaching and calling his disciples from there to his performing signs and wonders, he is clearly announcing his kingdom. People are believing on him and coming to saving faith. Another way of saying this is that he was building his church.

Think symbolically for one more minute. Imagine the light/darkness contrast when it comes to the thing that Caesarea Philippi was known for prior to the announcement of the kingdom of God—it was known as the doorway into the kingdom of darkness. How perfect a segue for a wordsmith like Christ. Of course he would announce that the kingdom of God would displace the kingdom of darkness on the very spot where the false gods of the underworld come and go through the swirling waters of a bottomless abyss. The false gods of this world are warned to flee from the approaching Light. It does not seem a stretch to imagine Jesus, when announcing that he would build his church on this rock, instead of looking at Peter, turned his gaze in the direction of the cave where images of Pan, Echo, and Hermes clung to the side of the hill, and warned them, "And the Gates of Hades will not prevail against it!"

This allows the path to remain even less cluttered for the fulfillment of the Rock, upon which the church would be built, to be Christ. The vision of the Rock in Daniel, which was not hewn from a mountain by a human hand, would tumble downhill and strike the great empires of the world during the dissolvement of Rome into a multiplicity of empires. That rock is the advancement of the kingdom of God, which advances out of the mouth of Jesus and out of his riven side. Every believer is a stone upon which more of the church is built; but only Christ is the Rock that can shoulder the kingdom in its entirety, advancing it by his Spirit into a hostile world, buckling the gates of the tenant deities.

Chapter 16

I Love Thy Kingdom, Lord

(Timothy Dwight, 1801)

I love thy kingdom, Lord, the house of thine abode:
The Church our blest Redeemer saved with His own precious blood.

I love thy Church, O God! Her walls before Thee stand,
Dear as the apple of thine eye, and grace on thy Hand.

For her my tears shall fall; for her my prayers ascend;
To her my cares and toils be given, til toils and cares shall end.

Beyond my highest joy I prize her heavenly ways,
Her sweet communion, solemn vows, Her hymns of love and praise.

Sure as thy truth shall last, to Zion shall be given
The brightest glories Earth can yield, and brighter bliss of Heaven.

Chapter 17

When it was evening, there came a rich man from Arimathea, named Joseph, who also was a disciple of Jesus. He went to Pilate and asked for the body of Jesus. Then Pilate ordered it to be given to him. And Joseph took the body and wrapped it in a clean linen shroud and laid it in his own new tomb, which he had cut in the rock. And he rolled a great stone to the entrance of the tomb and went away. Mary Magdalene and the other Mary were there, sitting opposite the tomb. (Matt 27:57–61)

AT THE VERY BEGINNING of the life of Christ, an innkeeper apologizes to Joseph and Mary that there are no more rooms in the house for them, but if they were willing, they could dwell with the animals in the stable that many historians and archaeologists agree would have been carved from the side of a hill or rock. At the very end of the life of Christ, we find him placed, yet again, in a rock tomb. This interaction between Joseph of Arimathea and Jesus offers up a representation of some of the riches to be found in Christ, namely union with him and the impotence of death over the believer.

At what many saw as the end of Jesus' life, Joseph of Arimathea took the body and wrapped it in a clean linen shroud. Joseph's linen shroud has long been surrounded by legend and controversy. The most reliable and weighty contribution of Joseph of Arimathea to the history of the church, however, is not the cloth in which Christ was wrapped, but the stone tomb in which his body was housed. Throughout this book, the question has been whether or not there is discernible literary coherence between many of the uses of rock and stone throughout Scripture, including this one. If so, the themes which have been identified so far should be recognized in this passage, or not.

John 19 informs us that Joseph was a rich man. He, similar to Nicodemus, seems to have been a secret follower of Jesus because he feared the personal ramifications of being openly associated with the controversial teacher. Here, he conquers that fear. Joseph is a wealthy man and personally requests the body of Christ from Pilate. This request is granted.

Even prior to the crucifixion, Jesus was counted among thieves and bandits. It was for this very reason, to fulfill the prophecies about being associated with criminals, that he orders his men to bring swords if they have them.

> He said to them, "But now let the one who has a moneybag take it, and likewise a knapsack. And let the one who has no sword sell his cloak and buy one. For I tell you that this Scripture must be fulfilled in me: 'And he was numbered with the transgressors.' For what is written about me has its fulfillment." And they said, "Look, Lord, here are two swords." And he said to them, "It is enough." (Luke 22:36–38)

There is a marked shift that occurs as soon as someone tries to use one of the swords the disciples were told to bring. In fact, Peter is rebuked in front of everyone, and told that this way of life is bankrupt. Why is that? It is because an association with criminals was on Jesus' mind and not a right to bear arms. This is expressed even further when damage is done to Malchus with one of these swords, and Jesus undoes the damage caused by the disciple who didn't recognize the difference between form and content.

The Messiah was already noted as being a friend of sinners, but this final stroke would ensure that those who wanted to dismiss his death as a justified conclusion would have due cause. The tragedy, of course, is that this assessment *of* his death would keep them from the justification that was brought about *by* his death. So, his men bring swords and then aren't allowed to use them. He is executed between thieves, and buried with nobility. Both counts of association with the wicked are followed by the reality that his association is just that—merely association. In truth, he is sinless, nonviolent, and regal, despite what it looks like. This would show sinners the truth that they could approach him as they were, but they would be changed if they stayed with him.

> And they made his grave with the wicked and with a rich man in his death, although he had done no violence, and there was no deceit in his mouth. (Isa 53:9)

After his death, he is placed inside a tomb that is cut from a rock. In addition to being associated with the wealth of Joseph of Arimathea, there is an even more ancient association taking place. Two beginnings seem to find their end in this final chapter: one is the Garden of Eden, the other is the Nativity.

The Garden of Eden was the beginning of the human story. The sin that took place in it was the beginning of the world's brokenness. It is for this reason that Scripture refers to Christ as the "Final Adam" (1 Cor 15). He successfully obeyed God in a way the first Adam did not (Rom 5). He restored all that was broken in sin's undoing (Isa 11, Acts 10) and began a new line of creation, one that flowed from his own righteousness rather than the first Adam's transgressions (Eph 2).

We see the very first garden as a call being answered at the other end of the age. All that went wrong in that first garden is made right in the death of Christ, which takes place in a new garden, we are told. Joseph's tomb was located in the garden in Golgotha.

> Now in the place where he was crucified there was a garden, and in the garden a new tomb in which no one had yet been laid. (John 19:41)

Whether it is true or not, the church has long dealt with the suggestion that the tomb of Adam was located under the place where Christ was crucified. Some go so far as to suggest that the skull of Adam was exposed to the cross during the Earthquake that followed the death of Christ. These details need not be historical for the Eden/Golgotha connection to be sound.

However, it is not only Eden that finds its fulfillment in Golgotha, but Bethlehem as well. It is of some consequence that the names mentioned concerning this Golgothan garden are Joseph and Mary, but even greater is the connection between what sort of shelter surrounded Christ, just prior to his birth, and what sort of shelter surrounded Christ just after his death.

Justin Martyr references Isaiah 33 as speaking of Jesus' birth. This affirms that long-standing tradition that has held to the manger existing in a cave, not an English barn. We can undoubtedly recognize that it also speaks of his burial. His dwelling place shall not just be in *a* rock, but in *the* Rock.

> He will dwell on the heights; his place of defense will be the fortresses of rocks; his bread will be given him; his water will be sure. (Isa 33:16)

G. K. Chesterton builds on the necessity of understanding this concept, in order to grasp the literary bookends that are sketched for us in Scripture. In his book *The Everlasting Man*, an entire chapter is dedicated to the

Messiah being, by necessity, a Man whose life is marked by abiding in rock. Touching upon some of the symbolic import expressed in such an event, Chesterton remarks:

> Christ was obviously conceived as born in a hole in the rocks primarily because it marked the position of one outcast and homeless. Nevertheless it is true, as I have said, that the cave has not been so commonly or so clearly used as a symbol as the other realities that surrounded the first Christmas. And the reason for this also refers to the very nature of that new world. It was in a sense the difficulty of a new dimension. Christ was not only born on the level of the world, but even lower than the world. The first act of the divine drama was enacted, not only on no stage set up above the sightseer, but on a dark and curtained stage sunken out of sight; and that is an idea very difficult to express in most modes of artistic expression. It is the idea of simultaneous happenings on different levels of life. Something like it might have been attempted in the more archaic and decorative medieval art. But the more the artists learned of realism and perspective, the less they could depict at once the angels in the heavens and the shepherds on the hills, and the glory in the darkness that was under the hills. Perhaps it could have been best conveyed by the characteristic expedient of some of the medieval guilds, when they wheeled about the streets a theater with three stages one above the other, with heaven above the earth and hell under the earth. But in the riddle of Bethlehem it was heaven that was under the earth.[1]

What is being taught to us, in the event of our Lord's body being placed in the tomb? What is the lesson? In addition to bookending the major beginnings already mentioned (Eden and Bethlehem), it hearkens to an important doctrine as well, that of the believer's union with Christ.

God has been consistently identified as the Rock of Defense, the Rock of Offense, the Rock of Refuge, and the Rock of Salvation. When we think biblically about Christ, whose birth and death were both framed inside a rock, we must never dismiss the symbolism of such an event as mere details. It is not pedantic to suck marrow from the bone. To be entombed in the rock is to say, "he is safe in God." We repeat such a phrase at the funeral of every believer—because of their union with Christ.

Joseph is wealthy. He gives of his wealth to Christ as an act of worship, not only the tomb, but spices as well. This, in fulfillment of the Isaiah

---

1. Chesterton, *The Everlasting Man*, 169.

passage concerning his death, affirms the parallelism again, because it was the magi who gave of their wealth in his birth; in their case, gold and spices.

It would be understandable to imagine that Joseph was giving his tomb to Christ, and not simply lending. The only people who seem to remember that Jesus promised to rise from the grave after three days were the Pharisees, and they secure the grave because of it. The truth is that Jesus does not need the tomb any longer than three days.

Jesus is buried in the rock. Because he emerges from the grave, he renders the use of the tomb no longer necessary. The vehicle for the doctrinal truth has been used and can be abandoned. The truth is still true. Christ is so secure in the Father that his body in the rock would be one of the last object lessons he would give to Earth on the matter. Since Joseph had received a saving faith from the Lord, he would give the Lord his wealth. After three days, Jesus leaves the tomb, but by leaving it via resurrection, he forever changes Joseph's relationship with the grave. Jesus was safe in the Father. Joseph, and every believer after him, is safe in Christ, who is safe in the Father. Because of the believer's union with him, it is as if the tomb had been rendered unnecessary to Joseph as well.

The death of the believer should be devoid of fear. Why? Because Christ was placed in the rock, and believers are placed in Christ. Scripture teaches we are raised with him in his resurrection because we have been buried with him in a death like his (Rom 6). The grave of Christ is a safe place in the symbolic lexicon of Israel, because it was in the Rock. So it is with the believer. This death is one that is to be seen as safe within the context of the sovereignty of God. The only altercation we will have with death is with its shadow (Ps 23). The fighter is not hurt during a shadow boxing bout. This is good news. In the truest sense, death should seem rather harmless:

> For you have died, and your life is hidden with Christ in God.
> (Col 3:3)

The final question is whether or not the prophetic Scriptures of Isaiah 53 are being fulfilled in this greater sense, in regards to Joseph's sharing of his tomb? Is it true that Christ reciprocates and shares his own wealth with Joseph (and every other believer for that matter)? We remember Isaiah 53:9 was fulfilled by Joseph giving his tomb to Christ. Notice how in the following verses (10–12), the Messiah is portrayed as sharing his own treasure with all those transgressors for whom he suffered—the very offspring that is counted as part of his wealth.

> Yet it was the will of the Lord to crush him; he has put him to grief; when his soul makes an offering for guilt, he shall see his offspring; he shall prolong his days; the will of the Lord shall prosper in his hand. Out of the anguish of his soul he shall see and be satisfied; by his knowledge shall the righteous one, my servant, make many to be accounted righteous, and he shall bear their iniquities. Therefore I will divide him a portion with the many, and he shall divide the spoil with the strong, because he poured out his soul to death and was numbered with the transgressors; yet he bore the sin of many, and makes intercession for the transgressors. (Isa 53:10–12)

In light of this, it is easy to imagine, as he approached the grave, how nourishing Christ must have found the Scriptures that proclaim God to be the Rock of Refuge. Clearly, from his final word on the cross, He knew he was going to the Father. He knew he was going to be secure in the hands of God in a moment. In Amos, God promises that evildoers who fall into the grave fall directly into his hand; how much more is this wonderfully true of Christ and his followers who are declared righteous because of his righteousness?

> If they dig into Sheol, from there shall my hand take them. (Amos 9:2a)

Joseph of Arimathea, in the company of the magi before him, gives to Christ his wealth and spices. He secures a place for Christ to abide in the rock, just as that long-ago innkeeper, unbeknownst to him, secured a place for Christ in the rock. The believer who abides in Christ, is secure because of his or her union with the Christ who abides in the Father. This is given to us by faith in the person and work of the Son of God. This is portrayed to us in the tomb in the garden of Golgotha. Christmas is the remembrance of Christ and his movement from the cradle to the grave—from cave to cave.

Cradled in a Manger, Meanly

(George S. Rowe, 1879)

Cradled in a manger, meanly,
Laid the Son of Man His head;
Sleeping His first earthly slumber
Where the oxen had been fed.
Happy were those shepherds listening
To the holy angel's word;
Happy they within that stable
Worshipping their infant Lord.
Happy all who hear the message
Of His coming from above;
Happier still who hail His coming,
And with praises greet His love.
Blessèd Savior, Christ most holy,
In a manger Thou didst rest;
Canst Thou stoop again, yet lower,
And abide within my breast?

Chapter 18

As it is written, "Behold, I am laying in Zion a stone of stumbling, and a rock of offense; and whoever believes in him will not be put to shame." (Rom 9:33)

THERE IS A PHOTOGRAPH from 2005 of a rockslide that took place in the Topanga Canyon, in California. In the famous picture, there is a boulder that fell into the road as the soil was being washed away by days of rain. The rock fills both lanes of the road perfectly, and is big enough to demand a long and laborious process of clearing the road for travel. There is no way to get around it. If our passage from Romans were getting ready to have *its* picture taken, we could ask the cameraman to leave everything as it is in the Topanga Canyon and just take one more picture. This passage is about a Rock that seems so poorly placed that it incites responses of either stumbling or being offended. The Rock in question is seen in one passage as being a solitary source of refuge in a storm. It is intended as a cornerstone, on which people are to build, but most reject the idea outright. There is the rock, and there is the rain pounding down on it. The line of cars, anxious to get around this rock, are laying on their horns and yelling out the window. Somebody do something. Move this thing. This Rock, we are told, is Jesus.

Paul employs the phrase "As it is written" in accordance with an ancient tradition. He is citing Scripture. It is the word of God that is telling us about a Stone being placed with great intention. There is a plan that God is hatching and the Stone is central. The quotation in Romans seems most likely to be a paraphrase of Isaiah 28:16, but there is something about the Silent Builder who places the Stone that also casts our minds to Psalm 118.

Paul is clearly preaching from Isaiah as his main text. Earlier in the chapter, he has quoted from Hosea as well, as he glances at some pages in Israel's photo album that are less than flattering. He is remembering the former days of their unbelief, and he is saying that this lack of faith is a legacy that has finally caught up with them. Gentiles, historically seen as unbelievers, have become the people of God simply by believing. This is not news. It was foretold by Isaiah in the very chapter Paul cites; the specific verse from which he quotes is verse 16:

> Therefore thus says the Lord GOD, "Behold, I am the one who has laid as a foundation in Zion, a stone, a tested stone, a precious cornerstone, of a sure foundation: 'Whoever believes will not be in haste.'" (Isa 28:16)

The context of the Isaiah passage is that God is accusing Ephraim and Jerusalem of great wickedness. He is telling them that there is a judgment that is coming upon them. Interestingly, the judgment is God, himself. He then describes himself, or this One who will come from him, as a hailstorm and a flood of mighty waters:

> Behold, the Lord has one who is mighty and strong; like a storm of hail, a destroying tempest, like a storm of mighty, overflowing waters, he casts down to the earth with his hand. (Isa 28:2)

The iniquity of Israel is like a scene from a biography on Epicurus. The priests who are supposed to be catechizing the children are so drunk that their vomit has covered the entire Sunday school table. There isn't even a clean spot on which to set the catechism. God is so disgusted with their abdication of their responsibilities that he prophesies a day in which a remnant of believers will be taught by people who speak a foreign tongue. The very idea is an offense to such an ethnocentric people. We are told that this will all take place right around the time that God himself stands up in the market and offers rest to those who are weary and heavy-laden, but they will have none of it.

> For by people of strange lips and with a foreign tongue the Lord will speak to this people, to whom he has said, "This is rest; give rest to the weary and this is repose"; yet they would not hear. (Isa 28:11–12)

Paul is preaching the gospel of Jesus Christ, and so Isaiah 28 is the perfect passage from which to preach. Unbelief is a bullseye at which the storm of judgment will take aim. Neither Paul, nor Isaiah, nor Jesus are excited about this; on the contrary, they lament it. They mourn it. They are heartbroken over it.

The source of contention is this ancient Stone. We are told that those who believe on him (the Stone) will not be put to shame or shaken easily. Isaiah says it is belief that is required; Paul, however, in line with progressive revelation, teaches that the Rock is Christ. Contrastingly, we are also told that it is this Rock that causes so many to stumble, to be offended, and to be put to shame—at least, those who do not believe on him.

From whence cometh this Stone? From God himself. God says that He, like a transcendent stonemason, is placing this Rock, presumably from heaven, directly in the center of his people, Zion. He does not stop there. He attributes certain characteristics to the Stone. It is for a specific purpose. It is not a generic stone; it is a stumbling Stone. It is not only a stumbling Stone, but it is also a foundation stone. According to Paul, there are two purposes ascribed to the Stone: to trip or offend some, and to be a foundation for others. This theme is recurrent in Paul's speaking of the ways in which Christ is rejected by both Greeks and Jews (1 Cor 1:23).

One winter a foot-long piece of wire had found its way from a bench in my garage into the front yard. A warm day followed by a cold day caused it to sink into the mud of the driveway and remain frozen in a thin loop, bound at both ends to the ground like a croquet wicket secured in concrete. It's color and thinness lent it all the necessary characteristics of a booby trap. I'm unsure how many people had been tripped by this little metal hoop, some falling, some stumbling, but all of them cursing me for not removing such a hazard sooner rather than later, before I finally got around to clipping it away. God is not avoiding the existence of just such a hazard in his dooryard. He has designed it. Not only has he designed it, but for those who do not trip over it, he would have them build their home on it. Hear how the psalmist speaks of this stone which the people of Zion have rejected.

> The stone that the builders rejected has become the cornerstone.
> (Ps 118:22)

This Stone that has caused countless to trip, and has offended so many, has become the cornerstone for others, per the ordination of God. This rejected Stone is decreed by God to be the perfect Stone. Every believer knows this to be true. All the ways in which Christ is offensive to the unbeliever are characteristics that inspire worship in the believer: his claim of being the only way to the Father; his confession of being the only effective vicarious means of redemption; his statement about being one with the Father; his declaration that he loves the world with compassion, but loves his people with a saving love. These claims are not accidentally offensive. It's not as though Jesus would go back and rephrase some of these statements and parables if he could, now that he knows how offended the crowds would be by them. Diplomacy doesn't seem to have any real estate on Jesus' hierarchy of needs. He is saying things in a manner that *ensures* they will offend. This isn't an accident; this is the plan of God.

> Then the disciples came and said to him, "Why do you speak to them in parables?" And he answered them, "To you it has been given to know the secrets of the kingdom of heaven, but to them it has not been given. For to the one who has, more will be given, and he will have an abundance, but from the one who has not, even what he has will be taken away. This is why I speak to them in parables, because seeing they do not see, and hearing they do not hear, nor do they understand. Indeed, in their case the prophecy of Isaiah is fulfilled that says: 'You will indeed hear but never understand, and you will indeed see but never perceive.' For this people's heart has grown dull, and with their ears they can barely hear, and their eyes they have closed, lest they should see with their eyes and hear with their ears and understand with their heart and turn, and I would heal them." (Matt 13:10–15)

The parables were employed to confuse people who were coming from a place of rebellion. This is far from what many would assume. Often, the thought is that Jesus used parables the way a politician uses a local example of his or her policies in action. If he's after the widest fanbase possible, then he should put everything under the lowest common denominator. Parables are much more complicated. The design is such that they will offensively confuse the unbeliever in order to establish them in their unrepentance, and they will often confound those called to faith, resulting in the necessity of curious hearers approaching the Lord for clarification. The result then is either repulsion or magnetism regarding the Lord, all based on whether faith is present or absent.

If we were to look at Psalm 118 for a moment, we would see that the context is the psalmist's rejoicing that God has decreed death not to have the final say. It is clearly messianic. It contains this running thread of life being triumphant over death, because of the will of God. The psalmist rejoices in the words which would later be sung by the children who praise the Christ during his triumphal entry into Jerusalem: "Blessed is he who comes in the Name of the Lord."

The Psalm 118 passage knits the event of the Cornerstone being placed by God with life's swallowing of death. This is, by necessity, speaking of the cross. It is on the cross that Christ's blood effectively paid for the sins of his people. It is on the cross that the wrath of the Father was satisfied. A short time later, the Holy Spirit is given and the breaking of ground commences on this global building project. This day is the day the Lord has crafted, the placing of the Stone in Zion. This is the day worthy of all rejoicing and praise. The true day to rejoice in was the day the Stone was laid in Zion for the people of God. The psalmist is not merely attempting to inspire praise in people for every day they wake up. Let us rejoice and be glad in that day as well; however, the true day in which the Scripture is enjoining us to rejoice is Good Friday:

> Open to me the gates of righteousness, that I may enter through them and give thanks to the Lord. This is the gate of the Lord; the righteous shall enter through it. I thank you that you have answered me and have become my salvation. The stone that the builders rejected has become the cornerstone. This is the Lord's doing; it is marvelous in our eyes. This is the day that the Lord has made; let us rejoice and be glad in it. (Ps 118:19–24)

The entire stanza of chapter 118 shows us more about the Stone. He is the central piece in the gates of righteousness being opened to the believer. He is crucially related to the way unto the Lord. This Stone, placed by God, is an answer to the believer's prayer for salvation. It is God's doing, and the day of this Stone's being placed by God is a day established by the will of God, and one worthy of all rejoicing and gladness.

And so it is that the two interpretations of the Stone are so different: either he inspires cursing or worship. Something in the middle is perhaps the worst kind of cursing. An old time preacher used to ask folks, "How's your walk with the Lord?" The most disturbing responses for him were the ones who said in Laodicean fashion, "Well, it's not hot, but it's not cold either." To not erupt in worship at the base of the Cornerstone simply means you haven't fully processed how you find him offensive.

And blessed is the one who is not offended by me. (Matt 11:6)

Coming back to the Isaiah passage with which we began, the judgment of God is promised to be administered. The promise was that if anyone believed on the Stone whom God was laying in Zion, they would not be shaken. In Romans, Paul has preached that Christ is the Stone. It's as though Jesus has this entire set design in his mind when he preaches the parable of the house built on the sand and the house built on the rock.

> Everyone then who hears these words of mine and does them will be like a wise man who built his house on the rock. And the rain fell, and the floods came, and the winds blew and beat on that house, but it did not fall, because it had been founded on the rock. And everyone who hears these words of mine and does not do them will be like a foolish man who built his house on the sand. And the rain fell, and the floods came, and the winds blew and beat against that house, and it fell, and great was the fall of it. (Matt 7:24–27)

Clearly, he is preaching on the same storm and the same rock as Isaiah. The storm is the judgment of God himself, and the Rock is Jesus. There are layers of application here. Immediately, in 70 AD, the judgment of God was poured out on Israel and, as Eusebius records, the Christians survived by hiding in a city named for its rock. Secondly, every human being must face the individual reality of either rejecting the Stone, or joyfully abiding in him. There is no other Rock, at least none that God has placed for his people, save this one.

Oh God, our Help in Ages Past

(Isaac Watts, 1719)

Our God, our help in ages past,
Our hope for years to come,
Be Thou our guard while troubles last,
And our eternal home.

Chapter 19

For I do not want you to be unaware, brothers, that our fathers were all under the cloud, and all passed through the sea, and all were baptized into Moses in the cloud and in the sea, and all ate the same spiritual food, and all drank the same spiritual drink. For they drank from the spiritual Rock that followed them, and the Rock was Christ. (1 Cor 10:1–4)

THE FIRST TIME I read these verses and understood them, I went back to the Old Testament and reread the passages on the Rock of Horeb in light of this Rock being Christ. Up until that time, I had only thought of typology as a few basic principles that applied to themes in the Old Testament like redemption and salvation finding their true fulfillment in Jesus. Even now, it is such a strange but edifying experience to read the book of Numbers with Christ as the silent and stolid protagonist being stricken in the center of the page.

Paul, although preaching in this letter on the Lord's Supper, and the differences between the two big covenants, teaches gospel believers how to go into the Old Testament and not view it like a ghost town. Any honest Bible reader will admit that between the covenants exists a consistent tension of continuity and discontinuity. The differences amongst Protestants has often been over the degree that one errs towards one of these poles.

This chapter is the one of the most instructive New Testament texts, when it comes to understanding a Biblical approach to feeding on the gospel in the Old Testament; however, before digging for gospel, we must understand the table manners that are being taught. In context, chapter 10 of 1 Corinthians is leading into the topic of communion, which climaxes in chapter 11. Paul is teaching New Covenant believers how to properly understand the ordinances. There are two ordinances or sacraments: baptism and communion. These are the two outward acts that bear witness to an inward reality of the participant having been born again of the Spirit of Christ. When the communicant partakes of the piece of bread, he is saying, "I'm a member of the Body of Christ" (1 Cor 11); that is why a single loaf is used. When the candidate is baptized, he is saying, "I have died to my old self and am born anew in Christ'" (Rom 6).

Paul is condemning the lack of integrity that existed in the unbelieving portion of Israel, despite the reality that they were communicants of the spiritual blessings. In the church, there are similar people who economically function like Christians, but are not actually believers. They participate in the ordinances, and share in the blessings, but disregard the censure given over falsely sharing in these outward professions and signs. This is why there is a warning given before the Lord's Supper, even in our own day. The caution that Paul issues in chapter 11 is to examine oneself and see if the profession that one gives, when participating in communion, is truly representative of one's own position in Christ. We take a sip of the wine, and we are saying, "his blood has had its way in me. I'm in the Covenant that is ratified in his blood." If none of this is true, the profession will end up being a witness that is called to the stand, on the day in which the defendant is tried and convicted. False or careless professions, like those sometimes given in communion and baptism, will one day appear and testify against the hypocrite.

Paul, remember, is preaching on the Lord's Supper, and he decides that the best place to make gospel sense of this issue would be to preach from Exodus and Numbers. It must be acknowledged that the road of understanding between the Old Testament and New Testament is a two-way street; having said that, the fulfillment of the Old Covenant is Christ. The covenant in his blood is new, and not like the old (Jer 31, Ezek 36). The primacy exists in the new as the interpretive lens, and not the other way around. The Old Testament speaks to the New Testament, but the foundation is Christ. This is counterintuitive, but a point that must be recognized—Christ is the foundation, not the patriarchs. The foundation stones of the Eternal City do not have the names of the twelve tribes of Israel on them; they have the names of the twelve apostles. We would expect that, because the twelve tribes came first, Jesus would build on top of them. But Jesus is the Cornerstone of the City, and it is all built on him. The twelve tribes are listed on the gates of the City, because that is how people entered in, but the newer twelve are the foundation (Ezek 48, Rev 21). Every true believer in the Old Covenant was panting after the New Covenant.

Israel is baptized into Moses, Paul says, when they passed under the cloud and through the sea. He uses the language of being "baptized into Moses" because Moses is clearly the Christ-figure, or the type, in this passage. He is the redeemer who is leading the people of God from captivity and bondage into rest. Jesus is the truer and greater Redeemer, delivering his people from truer and greater bondage than Egypt—namely, sin and death. Compared with the cross of Christ, the redemption that was accomplished in this Hebrew exodus is merely a tremor before the quake.

> Now I want to remind you, although you once fully knew it, that Jesus, who saved a people out of the land of Egypt, afterward destroyed those who did not believe. (Jude 1:5)

The cloud was over them, and the water was stacked on either side of them. The people were baptized by the water through which their trusted redeemer led them. Some of them followed Moses by faith; most followed defiantly. Moses led them through the water. This is the first point. Paul is saying that, in New Covenant terms, these Israelites were baptized folk.

The second point now emerges. Paul is talking to people who partake of the ordinances: baptism and the Lord's Supper. As we've seen, he portrays Israel of old as a people who have been baptized, and then he transitions into treating them as a people who also partook of spiritual food. In the New Covenant, this would be communion. Paul is preaching backwards, or from right to left. He is beginning in the New Covenant and preaching the revealed gospel into the darkness of the mystery. It's not that the gospel is not present in the Old Testament; rather, it's that Christ, by inaugurating a better covenant, ran power lines into the Old Testament, so now the place is humming with light. It is for this reason that contextualization must begin in the New Testament, rather than the Old Testament.

What is the food of which Israel partook? This itself was a type of Christ: the bread from heaven. Manna. Moses promised that a prophet would come after him who was like him but greater than him (Deut 18). When Jesus has his disciples feed the five-thousand-plus congregants on the side of the hill, he portrays himself as a kind of Moses, or an antitype to which Moses was the type—providing bread from heaven for an enormous amount of people in the middle of nowhere. An even greater symbol of Christ exists scattered on the ground. He is the truer Manna. He is the Bread from Heaven.

> I am the living bread that came down from heaven. If anyone eats
> of this bread, he will live forever. And the bread that I will give for
> the life of the world is my flesh. (John 6:51)

Paul is setting up a warning for people to make sure they do not partake of the lesser bread unless they have truly partaken of the greater Bread, which is his Body. They should not partake of the wine unless they are washed in the Blood. Some preachers in the past have rightly noted that the priest would be moving in the right direction if, instead of holding the wafer above his head, he spread his empty arms toward the congregation when he made his proclamation that the Body of Christ was present. The true Body of Christ, as defined by Jesus, is not in the priest's hands, but seated in the pews behind him. The true Body of Christ is the congregation of believers, not the meal.

Israel's drink in Exodus and Numbers was water, but in the New Covenant it is wine. It must not be missed that the preeminence of the New Covenant over the Old Covenant exists in Jesus' very first miracle: the turning of water into wine. Christ is clearly a hinge upon which the economy of God's interaction with his people is turning. His first miracle foreshadowed the turning of the covenantal tide.

It is not God that is changing. It is the covenant that is changing. It is the same God, but a different contract. Different terms, kept in a different manner. Again, the new is different, and not like the old. That is why it is called "The New Covenant," and not "The Same Old Covenant You've Always Known, but Better." God has not changed. He is the Unhewn Rock. This is made clear by Paul in pointing out that the Rock at Horeb was actually Jesus himself. And he does not stop there. No only does he say that the Rock was Christ, but that it was the Rock that was following them.

A child, seated in the backseat of a car, watches the moon out her window on the long drive home. "Daddy," she says, "The moon is following us home." Every parent who has experienced this has had the moment of sweet reflection in which they pondered whether they should tell their child the truth about relative angles and relative size, or if they should smile and allow the child to be safe for just a bit longer in their innocent simplicity. "The moon," says the eager father, "is only a rock. It can't be following you because it would need to be a free agent, and rocks don't choose." Paul, apparently, is the other kind of parent.

As I've said, we are only examining the frame of a painting of the Lord's Supper. We have not begun to talk about the doctrine of ordinances—the

Lord's Supper specifically. We are looking at what the Scriptures teach us about the Rock. Since the Holy Spirit sees fit to reference God, over and over again, as the Rock, it would be good for us to understand the implications of this reference. What we find is the story of the gospel, over and over.

Like Francis Thompson's poem about the hound who chases the poet throughout his life, the Rock emerges as the originator of all salvation. He is responsible for his people having come upon an oasis in the desert. He is a God who does not change. Regardless of the covenant, he hates when people profess belief and yet deny his power to save. The message of the gospel—the person and work of Jesus to glorify God by saving sinners—is pregnant in the Rock. It gushes out in the form of physical salvation.

> They tested God in their heart by demanding the food they craved. They spoke against God, saying, "Can God spread a table in the wilderness? He struck the rock so that water gushed out and streams overflowed. Can he also give bread or provide meat for his people?" Therefore, when the Lord heard, he was full of wrath; a fire was kindled against Jacob; his anger rose against Israel, because they did not believe in God and did not trust his saving power. (Ps 78:18–22)

It not mere coincidence that a clear point emerges within a teaching passage on communion, concerning the Rock as Jesus. There is no suggestion that the Rock became Jesus when Moses' staff struck its side. There is no transubstantiation of Jesus existing as literal compressed silt. We know this because, in Exodus 17, God says that he will "Stand before you by the rock." The reality of Christ as the Rock is clarified by Scripture teaching us that it was the presence of God accompanying the rock. Thankfully, this carries light back into the New Testament context concerning communion. In what way is the bread and wine of communion the body and blood of Jesus? By his spiritual presence accompanying it; it is not anything more literal. Again, the literal body that is physically present in communion is the gathering of believers (1 Cor 12), bound together by his Spirit.

The story that Paul is telling, concerning the truth of the gospel in Exodus, is that the Rock was Jesus, and it was the Rock that was doing the following, not the people. We are left with no other option than to understand that, in addition to all the other layers of doctrine which are compounded in this relationship with the Rock at Horeb, election is also being taught.

The people of God did not go out and find a Rock from which to drink. The Rock followed them home and noticed they were thirsty.

The Hound of Heaven

(By Francis Thompson, 1859–1907)
Lines 155–182

Now of that long pursuit
Comes on at hand the bruit;
That Voice is round me like a bursting sea:
'And is thy earth so marred,
Shattered in shard on shard?
Lo, all things fly thee, for thou fliest Me!
Strange, piteous, futile thing!
Wherefore should any set thee love apart?
Seeing none but I makes much of naught' (He said),
'And human love needs human meriting:
How hast thou merited—
Of all man's clotted clay the dingiest clot?
Alack, thou knowest not
How little worthy of any love thou art!
Whom wilt thou find to love ignoble thee,
Save Me, save only Me?
All which I took from thee I did but take,
Not for thy harms,
But just that thou might'st seek it in My arms.
All which thy child's mistake
Fancies as lost, I have stored for thee at home:
Rise, clasp My hand, and come!'
Halts by me that footfall:
Is my gloom, after all,
Shade of His hand, outstretched caressingly?
'Ah, fondest, blindest, weakest,
I am He Whom thou seekest!
Thou dravest love from thee, who dravest Me.'

Chapter 20

As you come to him, a living stone rejected by men but in the sight of God chosen and precious, you yourselves like living stones are being built up as a spiritual house, to be a holy priesthood, to offer spiritual sacrifices acceptable to God through Jesus Christ. (1 Pet 2:4–5)

THINK, FOR A MOMENT, of children roasting marshmallows over a campfire. How often children will compete with one another to see who can brown the treat without blackening it. It is almost inevitable that most attempts will end in flames. As the sugar approaches the fire, a chemical reaction occurs, manifested in the changing of the color, texture, and even shape of the marshmallow. These verses of Peter's begin by describing a chemical reaction of sorts. As we come to Jesus, we, like something in his image, are shaped into something like a house for him. If the simile were comparing Christ and his people to fire, the verse would read something like, "As you come to him, a brilliant Fire rejected by men, but in the sight of God chosen and precious, you yourselves sort of burst into flames." But that is not how the text reads. Christ himself is a living Stone, rejected by men, and those who come to him, being made like him, are built up as something fit to house him.

There are a number of stops along the route of new birth. The process begins with regeneration. The word is self-explanatory. It is a new beginning, a new creature being born. Jesus says that it is new birth that is required before someone can even see the kingdom (John 3:3). Regeneration is a process that takes place in a person long before they ever willfully surrender to Christ. It needs to happen this way. We wouldn't even see the kingdom to long for it, or to choose it, if regeneration didn't precede justification.

J. I. Packer says that regeneration is like birth and sanctification is like growing.[1] In the above Scripture, Peter is showing that there is a change taking place as one comes to Christ. A person's coming to Christ could not happen apart from regeneration (Eph 2:1-8, Rom 8:29-30, 2 Tim 1:9). Two verses prior show that he is speaking to people who have already undergone newbirth:

> Like newborn infants, long for the pure spiritual milk, that by it
> you may grow up into salvation—if indeed you have tasted that the
> Lord is good. (1 Pet 2:2–3)

Regeneration being assumed, Peter goes on to say that, as one comes to Christ, he or she is changed into his image. This is sanctification. It can easily be understood that anyone who has yielded to Christ, but is not yet with him in all his fullness, in some way, is still coming to him. That is why he uses the language of growing into salvation after one has been born again. The Christian is both born again and yet growing. New creature, and yet still emerging—saved and being saved.

This theme of duality is captured by the writer of Hebrews as well:

> For by a single offering he has perfected for all time those who are
> being sanctified. (Heb 10:14)

But the chemical reaction does not only change us into his image, it commits us to his purposes. They will be done in those who are his, and some of them are expressly stated in this passage:

> Therefore thus says the Lord GOD, "Behold, I am the one who
> has laid as a foundation in Zion, a stone, a tested stone, a precious
> cornerstone, of a sure foundation: 'Whoever believes will not be in
> haste.'" (Isa 28:16)

And again, Isaiah:

> And he will become a sanctuary and a stone of offense and a rock
> of stumbling to both houses of Israel, a trap and a snare to the
> inhabitants of Jerusalem. (Isa 8:14)

These are the two passages that Peter is preaching. The consequence of Christ being laid as a stone is that we who are in Christ would be a priesthood who work day and night to glorify God. In the end, the sacrifice the priesthood offers up is a life of worship to this God, lived in such a way that

---

1. Packer, *Concise Theology*, 170.

it encourages and not discourages the worship of God by those who see our lives. This is Peter, saying what these verses mean:

> So the honor is for you who believe, but for those who do not believe, "The stone that the builders rejected has become the cornerstone," and "A stone of stumbling, and a rock of offense." They stumble because they disobey the word, as they were destined to do. But you are a chosen race, a royal priesthood, a holy nation, a people for his own possession, that you may proclaim the excellencies of him who called you out of darkness into his marvelous light. Once you were not a people, but now you are God's people; once you had not received mercy, but now you have received mercy. Beloved, I urge you as sojourners and exiles to abstain from the passions of the flesh, which wage war against your soul. Keep your conduct among the Gentiles honorable, so that when they speak against you as evildoers, they may see your good deeds and glorify God on the day of visitation. (1 Pet 2:7–12)

In all of this we remember back to the commandment in Exodus 20:25, that anything offered to God is to be offered on an altar of unhewn stone. It is not to be crafted according to our liking, nor shaped in our image, or projection of an image. We are not only the stones, but as Paul says in Romans 12, we are also the sacrifice on the stones. This does not deviate in any way from our Example. He was both Priest and Sacrifice. Being living stones means that every function of our being should be a sacrifice to God. Whatsoever our hands find to offer, we are offering it to God. It is for this reason that the marriage bed is undefiled, that whether we eat or drink we do it to God, and that our bodies and their functions should be offered to God as worship (Heb 13:4, 1 Cor 10:31, Rom 12:1).

What are we told about this Living Stone, in Whose Image all other living stones are created? We are told that he is both despised and loved: a living stone rejected by men but in the sight of God chosen and precious.

He is clearly the fulfillment of the Isaiah promise that he will be a sanctuary to some of Israel, but also a stone of offense, a rock of stumbling, a trap, and a snare to others. This is shown plainly in the memorializing of two different responses to Christ, in Matthew 26. Mary, the sister of Martha, commits a beautiful act of worship toward Christ, and Judas is so repulsed with Christ for not rejecting it that he rejects Christ.

> The disciples were indignant when they saw this. "What a waste!" they said. "It could have been sold for a high price and the money given to the poor." But Jesus, aware of this, replied, "Why criticize

this woman for doing such a good thing to me? You will always have the poor among you, but you will not always have me. She has poured this perfume on me to prepare my body for burial. I tell you the truth, wherever the Good News is preached throughout the world, this woman's deed will be remembered and discussed." Then Judas Iscariot, one of the twelve disciples, went to the leading priests and asked, "How much will you pay me to betray Jesus to you?" And they gave him thirty pieces of silver. From that time on, Judas began looking for an opportunity to betray Jesus. (Matt 26:8–16)

Here is where the two roads diverge. In absolute surrender and sacrifice, Mary worships Jesus with work of beauty. Jesus loves it. He promises to memorialize it and to have the whole world remember her worship. Shakespeare, in Sonnet 18, promises to memorialize a woman's beauty, but the point of wonder with which he is enraptured is his own power to memorialize. More than anything else, he praises himself and is remembered for it. No one remembers the name of the woman whose beauty he supposedly etched in eternity. The author does work to glorify creation. Mary does a work of beauty to adorn Jesus, and Jesus commemorates the worship as being worthy of remembrance. You will work to adorn something. You will strive to serve a cause—what cause will it be, making God known—or anything else? Judas is the person whose religion allows for Christ to be the motivation for ministry, but not the object of all our adoration.

What is this house into which we are being built? What could the building analogy even mean? If we were left with only an analogy, then it could be anyone's guess; but, we are given further enumeration. We are told directly that to be this house, specifically in this passage, means two things: that they are a holy priesthood, and they they are to offer spiritual sacrifices acceptable to God through Jesus Christ, to be a holy priesthood.

A priest is someone whose vocation and calling affect every area of their life. They don't clock out. They don't go certain places. They don't touch certain things. A priest is an intercessor between sinful humans and God. Every believer has been called into this service. This is not a description of clergy; not in the New Covenant. This is a description of Christians. The priesthood is holy, and it is comprised of everyone who comes to him as that Holy Foundation, to offer spiritual sacrifices acceptable to God through Jesus Christ.

This second and final thing that it means to be living stones made into a house for the Living Stone is to offer certain kinds of sacrifices in a certain kind of way. These New Covenant priests are to offer spiritual sacrifices, and ones that are acceptable to God through Jesus Christ. What does it mean to offer spiritual sacrifices, and how do I know whether God will accept them or not?

A spiritual sacrifice is one that goes deeper than the body and the soul. If one can imagine the body as housing the appetites, and the soul as housing intellect and personality, then the spirit is where the breath of life is housed. Spiritual sacrifices are to be ones that go deeper than that which can be concocted. A spiritual sacrifice is offered from a place where the personality has been unable to tamper with it. It is viscerally and dependently offered in surrender. Judas paid lip service to Jesus, in some way. He was a follower and a disciple. Unlike Joseph of Arimathea and Nicodemus who were disciples of Jesus secretly, Judas was an apostate secretly. Mary, on the other hand, potentially, dumped her dowry on Jesus' head. She washed the filth off his feet with her hair, which Scripture refers to as her "glory" (1 Cor 11:15). Her sacrifice was accepted because it was spiritual, not because it was creative. This means that her sacrifice was in line with that of Abel, whose gift was accepted because it was given in faith, which can be understood as dependence and trust. A spiritual sacrifice is given as something that had been given to the worshiper. As one of the doxologies says, "We give Thee but Thine own, whate'r the gift may be" (William W. How, 1823–1897).

> By faith Abel offered to God a more acceptable sacrifice than Cain, through which he was commended as righteous, God commending him by accepting his gifts. And through his faith, though he died, he still speaks. (Heb 11:4)

To offer these sacrifices, by faith, in a manner that is acceptable to God, they must be offered in truth. Truthful and spiritual worship is the kind of worship that God accepts, through Jesus. When we exalt Christ, the Father is receiving worship through it, but we must speak truth and speak it truthfully. God does not need singers. He does not look at the congregation mumbling words to which they are hardly paying attention, whose minds are on the football game they're missing, and think to himself, "Well, at least they're singing."

> But the hour is coming, and is now here, when the true worshipers will worship the Father in spirit and truth, for the Father is seeking such people to worship him. (John 4:23)

What does a living stone look like? In order to answer that with any finality, we must look at the Prototype. A living stone is a thing rejected by men, but in the sight of God chosen and precious. In that phrase, we see the holiness of the priesthood and the acceptance of a sacrifice pleasing to God. What was the sacrifice of The Living Stone? It was his life: his living and his dying. In theology, it is called the active and passive obedience of Christ. He did not only die in a manner that was acceptable and pleasing to God, but he lived that way as well. It is in that little dash between the two dates on your headstone, as preachers like to say, that living sacrifices are offered. Not living to do the work of ministry, but living to the glory of God. Adorning the beauty of Christ with absolutely anything we have, especially our dependence and need.

Bibliography

Andrews, Adam. "The Seeing of the Eye." *Circe* no. 5 (2017) 23.

Adler, Mortimer. *How to Read a Book*. New York: Touchstone, 1972.

Augustine. *The Anti-Pelagian Writings*. Charleston, SC: Createspace, 2015.

Brown, Francis. *The Brown-Driver-Briggs Hebrew and English Lexicon*. Peabody, MA: Hendrickson, 1994.

Chesterton, G. K. *The Everlasting Man*. San Francisco, CA: Ignatius, 1993.

Edersheim, Alfred. *Sketches of Jewish Social Life*. New York: James Pott, 1876.

Ellul, Jacques. *The Humiliation of the Word*. Grand Rapids, MI: Eerdmans, 1985.

Green, Melody. *No Compromise*. Nashville, TN: Thomas Nelson, 1982. Kindle edition.

Grudem, Wayne. *Systematic Theology*. Grand Rapids, MI: Zondervan, 1994.

Jamieson, Robert, et al. *Commentary on the Whole Bible*. Hartford, CT: S. S. Scranton, 1871.

Josephus. *Antiquities Book III*. Grand Rapids, MI: Kregel, 1960.

Josephus. "Of the War—Book III." http://penelope.uchicago.edu/josephus/war-3.html.

Keller, Tim. *The Prodigal God*. New York: Penguin, 2008.

Law, Henry. *The Gospel in Exodus*. Charleston, SC: Createspace, 2017.

Miller, Jack. *Sonship*. Greensboro, NC: New Growth, 2013.

Packer, J. I. *Concise Theology: A Guide to Historic Christian Beliefs*. Carol Stream, IL: Tyndale, 1993.

Schaeffer, Francis. *Joshua*. Downers Grove, IL: IVP, 1974.

Schaff, Philip. *The Creeds of Christendom Volume III*. Grand Rapids, Michigan: Baker, 1990.

Spurgeon, C. H. "Ebenezer." *Spurgeon Gems*. www.spurgeongems.org/vols7-9/chs500.pdf.

Tozer, A. W. *The Knowledge of the Holy*. New York: HarperCollins, 1960.